BROTHERHOOD OF THE BAG

A Wholesaler's Handbook

BROTHERHOOD OF THE BAG

A Wholesaler's Handbook

ROB SHORE

ISBN-13: 978-0-9890580-0-1
ISBN-10: 0-9890580-0-X

Editor: Catherine Leek of Green Onion Publishing
Electronic Page Design and Composition: Kim Monteforte,
    WeMakeBooks.ca
Front Cover Design: Kim Monteforte, WeMakeBooks.ca

To all those, who knowingly or unknowingly,
provided the inspiration and education necessary
to write this book — thank you.

CONTENTS

About the Word "Brotherhood" xv

Introduction xvii

How to Use this Book xxi

Part
One

THE WONDER YEARS

You Gotta Get Your Teeth Kicked In 1

Your Best Client Is Their Best Prospect 3

Are You a Wholesaling Pretender? 6

Nobody Works Past 5 O'Clock 9

Virgins Wanted 10

TMT — The Only Thing a Wholesaler Has to Offer 12

They Call Me Termite Terry 14

*Why Wholesaling Is Like Roofing Tiles,
Only Different* 16

The Purpose of Repurposing — From the
Department of Redundancy Department 18

Gimme Pastrami on Rye 21

How to Craft a Story and Spin It 24

Do You Give Good Phone? 28

How to Butcher a Prospect 30

How Much Love Should Wholesalers Give to
Top Producers? 32

8 Ounces of Water Worth $5,000? 33

And the Wholesaler Said, "Enough About Me,
Let's Talk About Me." 35

The Allure of the Filler Appointment 37

Run Your Business Like a Business, Not a Clubhouse ... 38

Do You Get Dirty in Your Territory's Data? 40

Simple, Not Easy 41

76 Great Questions Wholesalers Should
Ask Advisors 43

10 Ways Wholesalers Can Increase Their Likeability ... 48

8 Ways Wholesalers Succeed with COIs 52

8 Ways Wholesalers Can Improve Their
Presentation Skills 55

14 Guaranteed Ways to Achieve Success with Your
Internal Wholesaler 59

Sometimes I'm Not Too Bright 62

5 Things to Not Do at Your Next Conference 63

9 What Ifs: A Wholesaler's Approach to Working
Conferences 65

Brief and Occasional Train Noise 66

Part Two

INCREASING YOUR MQ — MEMORABILITY QUOTIENT®

Deciding Between 4½ and 4½ 69

Legends and Four-Legged Friends 72

What Side of the Bed Do You Sleep on? 73

The Legend of 9D 76

You're Invited: Wholesaler Pool Party 79

The Door Is Wide Open, So Why Aren't Wholesalers
    Walking Through It? 81

Just One Great Sales Idea 83

How Wholesalers Build Confidence by Developing
    Their PVP — Peerless Value Proposition® 84

7 Ways Wholesalers Can Market Like Coca-Cola 86

The Lowest Paying White-Collar Job 89

The Typical Wholesaler vs the Great Wholesaler —
    An Infographic 91

Welcome to the Wholesaler Beauty Pageant 94

Wholesalers Should Never Show Advisors
    Their Sixth Toe 96

A Wholesaler's Second Chance 98

The Four Cs of the Legendary Wholesaler 101

Undeniable Attributes of the Greatest Wholesalers ... 104

They Made the Cable Company Look Good 109

3 Things Wholesalers Do to Impress Home
  Office Visitors 110

CEO, Oh No! 112

5 Things to Do to Make COIs Love You 114

Go Lie Down 117

23 Client Event Ideas for Wholesalers to Use
  with Advisors 119

20 Great Ideas Wholesalers Use to be More
  Productive — and Memorable 124

5 Ways Wholesalers Develop More Openable and
  Readable Emails 128

Let the Haters Hate 132

8 Ways Wholesalers Can Best Use Voice Mail
  as a Sales Tool 134

Is Your Internal Pitch Perfect 136

Part
Three

FOR GREAT WHOLESALERS'
EYES ONLY

Laila Wanted Me Fired 139

Not Cut Out for Wholesaling 142

Tell Me Where It Hurts: Business Planning with
  Financial Advisors 144

The One Question Ticking Off Advisors 146

Advanced Wholesaler Technique: The Benefits
   of Forward Scheduling 148

   Lone Wolf Wholesaler 151

Wholesalers Shouldn't Neglect the Movable Middle ... 153

   One-Hit Wonders 154

Take the Less Traveled Wholesaling Road 156

   Yes, I Do Windows Too 157

Great Wholesalers: 8 Ways to Always Be Closing 159

Bud Fox Style Elephant Hunting 162

Time to Let a Few "F" Bombs Fly 165

   No Means No! 168

Hold Me Closer, Tony Danza 170

How Valuable Is Candid Feedback? 172

   Sympathy Is a Wasted Emotion 174

One Completely Ridiculous Reason Advisors
   Tune Wholesalers Out 176

   Mr. Magoo Must Be a Long-Lost Relative of Mine 178

Wholesaling Chicken or Wholesaling Egg? 179

4 Things Advisors Need from Wholesalers in
   Challenging Markets 182

21 Ways Wholesalers Can Shorten the Sales
   Cycle with Advisors 185

10 Ways to Ignite the Fuse with a Producer 188

   Catsup or Ketchup — It's Still Heinz 190

3 Ways Wholesalers Can Have More Productive
   Advisor Meetings 192

Part
Four

WILL YOU SURVIVE THE
WHOLESALING MARATHON?

Are You an Automatic? 195

The Wholesaling Marathon 197

A Lot More than 10 Rules for Wholesalers 199

*Everywhere Is Walking Distance If You Have
the Time* 202

Wholesalers: What Style of Communicator
Is Your Sales Manager? 203

Sushi, Sake, See Ya 205

Some Wholesalers Are Like Stale Real Estate Listings ... 208

The Croissant 210

Confessions of a Wholesaling Workaholic 212

Time to Do My Nails 213

The One About the Spineless Wholesaler 215

What Are the 5 Drivers of Wholesaler
Dissatisfaction? 217

Can Wholesaler Ego and Humility Live Side by Side? ... 221

When Did You Stop Learning? 223

The Powder Blue Wall Phone 224

Good News! I Got Fired and I'm Leaving
Wholesaling 226

3 Questions to Ask Yourself 228

20 Questions Wholesalers Should Ask Themselves
to Have a Career Year 230

11 Things Wholesalers Must Do to Ensure a Long
and Successful Career 232

Pool Man Jumped the Shark, So I Fired Him 238

14 Essential Wholesaling Skills Your Manager
Wants You to Have 240

15 Sales Rules to Live (and Die) By 248

Stiletto Heels and Power Washers 249

7 Ways Wholesalers Can Survive a Manager
Ride-Along Visit 251

12 Numbers for Wholesalers to Obsess About
Besides Production 254

5 Ways for Wholesalers to Cope with Feeling
Overwhelmed 256

6 Ways Wholesalers Become Franchise Players 260

8 Ways Great Wholesalers Prepare for Vacation 262

Confessions of a Hotel Snob 263

11 Reasons Great Wholesalers Leap Out of Bed
in the Morning 265

Conclusion 269

Your Picture of Success 269

About the Author 273

About the Cover 276

ABOUT THE WORD "BROTHERHOOD"

Back in the dark ages of distribution, I remember hearing the phrase "good ole boys club." It was most commonly referenced by women in the wholesaling community who observed that the lion's share of both frontline wholesalers and their leaders where overwhelmingly male.

Now some 30 years later, this has, fortunately, changed such that some of the most influential and successful members of the community are female.

The title of the book, *Brotherhood of the Bag*, is derived from the Merriam-Webster dictionary definition of "brotherhood" which says: *the whole body of persons engaged in a business or profession.*

Throughout the book the topic of wholesaling is referenced in a gender neutral fashion, alternating between both male and female references.

INTRODUCTION

It was the summer of 1987, a few weeks after completing my first few trades as a newly minted financial advisor at GNA Securities at Home Fed Bank. The phone rang and a friendly voice on the other end of the line said, "Hello, Rob. This is Diane with Franklin Funds."

And immediately my defenses went up.

Yes, defenses. Though Diane was a Franklin Funds wholesaler and she was calling to say thanks for the business and to schedule our first appointment, I was convinced that she was, in some subversive way, an extension of the Compliance Department. Not knowing that wholesalers even existed, I was sure she was going to scrutinize the suitability of the trades I had written.

Go ahead, call me paranoid.

Then, some months later, a new team of wholesalers started working with our broker/dealer from Kemper Funds. It was through a relationship with one of those wholesalers that I began to see the career path I wanted my financial services profession to take.

But making the jump to wholesaling was no easy feat. Over the course of the next two years, I was promoted to a managerial role and had a chance to visit the home offices of the fund companies with which we did business. These visits reinforced my resolve to get into Distribution.

Resolute in knowing that representing products to the public customer was just not my calling (if I had to explain the inverse relationship of interest rates to bond prices one more time I'd implode), I began the full-court press to become a wholesaler.

It started down the most obvious path — speaking to the divisional and national sales managers our firm did business with to explore their interest in hiring a rookie like me. Fortunately, I had a direct line into these leaders, since I was a Center of Influence for them, and my inquiries were met with a cordial reception.

Cordial, polite, and filled with wholesaler hiring manager code. The code wherein the manager says, "We'll definitely keep you in mind" — which translates to, "You don't have a snowball's chance!"

It was time to ramp up the search and to do so in a more aggressive fashion.

The annual *Forbes Mutual Funds* edition had just come out, and in the early 1990s the issue was filled with all the data I needed to start cold calling the firms that were in my sights. So one morning I quietly made my way behind closed doors and started to dial, alphabetically, the main numbers of the largest mutual fund companies.

A through D yielded nothing worth mentioning. When I got to the Es, I reached the national sales manager at Eaton Vance. I was encouraged simply because he had an opening and didn't slam the telephonic door in my face/ear. While he offered to look at my resume, I sensed that I should keep dialing.

Upon reaching the Os, and now 15 letters into my dial-a-thon, I was ready for something good to happen. The receptionist at OppenheimerFunds connected me with a woman named Maryann Bruce. She explained that she was just starting a new division for the firm that was going to focus on a new segment of their distribution strategy — Banks.

She said she was looking for someone to cover eight western states who:

- had established connections with senior management at bank broker/dealers,
- had prior experience wholesaling mutual funds, and
- knew the bank marketplace.

I thought, "Well, one out of three isn't bad."

After going into full sales mode explaining why I was her man, in spite of the less than ideal fit, she requested my resume, which I made sure landed on her desk the next morning. We spoke shortly thereafter and, as she was on her way out for maternity leave, made arrangements for me to meet the President of the distributor, Jim Ruff, who would be interviewing a slew of candidates in Los Angeles.

My memory of that interview is blurred by nerves and anticipation. But I can tell you about one statement that Jim made that would set the stage for my future in our business.

He said, "Rob, you do understand that OppenheimerFunds will own you Monday through Friday, right?"

What he failed to mention was that this job, career, lifestyle owns us 24 hours a day and all 7 days of the week!

And so in December 1991, I attended my first advisor meeting as a wholesaler with OppenheimerFunds.

Why this Book?

Brotherhood of the Bag is an extension of the work that I do every day in the wholesaling community. A community, that until the inception of WholesalerMasterminds.com, had no central place to digitally gather and get filled up with ideas and best practices to consider when seeking to improve (or simply reality check) their own wholesaling practices.

Assembled in this book are the very best content bytes, gathered from over five years of content creation — all dedicated to making you a better practitioner of your craft.

HOW TO USE
THIS BOOK

Within each chapter of the book you'll find three component pieces.

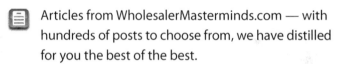 Articles from WholesalerMasterminds.com — with hundreds of posts to choose from, we have distilled for you the best of the best.

Applicable Sunday Night Emails — now in its third year, our email goes out to over 10,000 wholesalers around the globe every single week. In this book, you'll find some of the most read and most commented upon pieces that we've sent.

Relevant lists — anytime a list appears in Wholesaler Masterminds it gets a ton of clicks. Here we have assembled the most popular lists to assist you.

I invite you to highlight, circle, bookmark, or otherwise notate the heck out of this handbook.

Because it was written for you.

Part One

THE WONDER YEARS

You Gotta Get Your Teeth Kicked In

At OppenheimerFunds, I spent a ton of time training future bank platform reps to sell mutual funds for Cal-Fed Bank (may they rest in peace).

Each month, the Mutual Funds One class would begin with participant introductions. From the wide eyes and hesitant voices, I could tell that these new Account Representatives were not quite ready to embark on the company mandate — selling non-deposit products to bank clients.

By day three, after filling their brains with an inordinate amount of information, but before turning them loose on the investing public, I asked them about their level of confidence.

Most replied that they were worried — worried about sounding or looking bad.

I reminded them that everyone starting out must "get their teeth kicked in."

They needed to risk looking/sounding less than perfect (or even downright foolish) the first few times they made a presentation in order to have any hope of becoming a great investment sales professional.

And changing the way you wholesale is no different.

As we go to press on *Brotherhood of the Bag,* we mourn the passing of an icon — Wonder Bread. Produced for 90+ years, this was the carbohydrate staple of lunchtime sandwiches and family dinner tables throughout the land. In the 1960s, Wonder's ad campaign touted that it "Builds Strong Bodies" in young people, and it coined the phrase "The Wonder Years."

Owing to that reference, the latter-day version of the phrase was used to depict the coming-of-age TV series in the late 1980s.

And now we borrow The Wonder Years to depict the formative time in a wholesaler's life where they will either build the strong bodies that endure a career's worth of wholesaling wear and tear or form bad habits that will derail their well-intended destination — becoming a wholesaling great.

Know this though, regardless of how long you have been wholesaling, I'll bet you have had this thought: you are screaming down the freeway and mentally reviewing the results of the day when you realize that what you knew about our business and your practice six months ago (or a year ago, or five years ago) pales in comparison to what you know today. In fact, you may even say to yourself, "What was I thinking! How could I have believed that idea, process, or approach was worthwhile?"

In this section, we will review the nitty-gritty of wholesaling. Each story in this section is designed to make you think about the core of what you do and how you will create sustainable success as a great professional wholesaler.

 ## Your Best Client Is Their Best Prospect

I'm Rob, and I'm a recovering United Airlines Million Miler.

What have they done to wrong me?

Nothing.

It's what another has done to court and impress me.

This week, I had the great fortune of traveling to conduct a 3-hour workshop at an elite meeting of 80 of the best wholesalers of a tier-one distributor.

I booked Delta as they had the best connections along with adult size aircraft — I avoid regional jets at all costs.

Thirty minutes before takeoff, the gate agent apologetically told the packed gate area that there was a mechanical issue and departure time was pushed out 45 minutes.

Knowing my connecting time in the megalopolis that is ATL was 41 minutes, this proved problematic.

With time to kill, I tweeted my dissatisfaction.

Minutes later @DeltaAssist tweeted back asking if they could help.

Meanwhile, I dialed the Delta Service Recovery Center 800 number provided to all, as my status on Delta, well, wasn't.

I braced for the worst.

Instead I got an agent on the first ring.

She rebooked me to the next later connecting flight.

Once airborne, I noticed that the pilot was exceeding the speed limit — thereby causing us to arrive only 10 minutes late.

Using in-flight Wi-Fi I sent @DeltaAssist a message, and they rebooked me back on the earlier flight and held the later one too.

Now I'm covered six ways from Sunday and my blood pressure never rose a point.

Impressive Delta.

What's your competition doing to court and impress your best clients? How are you responding?

Are You a Wholesaling Pretender?

Most of us fly a lot. If you're like me you usually read, listen to music, listen to air traffic control, or perhaps read and respond to email.

The idea is to avoid talking to the guy next to you.

However, every now and then a stranger is intriguing. Just the way he or she looks and carries him- or herself makes you want to learn more.

On a recent flight, a stately looking gentleman sat down in the seat next to me.

He was about 65 years old and was dressed like a British professor. You know the kind — houndstooth coat, bow tie, and a gray beard. I couldn't resist asking him what he did for a living.

He introduced himself as Professor (I was right!) Heinrick Von Saleby of The Hamburg Educational Institute of Wholesaler Higher Attainment Technology, otherwise known as THE WHAT?

He told me his life's work was analyzing wholesaler behavior and habits in the field.

Imagine my shock. I'm sitting next to an expert on the subject that is nearest and dearest to my heart.

I asked him, "What are critical areas that separate wholesaling greats from wholesaling pretenders?"

Here are three of the many he spoke of.

Professor Von Saleby had coined the phrase "Pontificatus Excessus." In lay person's terms, it means "talk too much, listen too little."

Let's face it, there is only so much information that you can offer regarding your product. After the thorough overview, followed by the in-depth analysis, then what are you going to discuss?

Visiting a rep for the first time requires deft skill, not unlike a physician in the diagnosis phase.

What is the advisor's mix of business, goals for this year, target markets, challenges in the branch, areas they wish they could improve, career goals?

The professor has calculated that the ratio of listen to talk needs to be in excess of 3 to 1, especially on that first call.

If you don't excel at the "discovery process," exactly what are you going to discuss on the next visit?

Now some of you may be thinking, "Gee, this professor has an amazing grasp of the obvious!" Yet I have to tell you that I still hear both financial advisors and Centers of Influence complain about this issue, and I've seen countless wholesalers in the field who are bent on only jamming product. No value created.

Another of the professor's traits that distinguish wholesalers is summed up in the phrase, "Wholesaler Consumed by Territory, Film at 11:00." The professor, exercising his acute sense of humor, asked me, "Who manages whom in the relationship between you and your territory?"

Are your weeks planned using a rotation structure or on the "well, she called so I'm there" method?

Don't laugh.

There are far too many wholesalers in the business who espouse the latter theory.

Properly planned weeks (rotations, loops) are an art form.

To know where you will be 8, 12, 16 weeks from now is not only efficient but makes scheduling (the bane of most wholesalers' existence) considerably easier. To walk out of an appointment with an activity planned for your next visit, at an agreed upon date, is both a great scheduling technique and impressive to the advisor.

The professor then spoke of a phenomenon called "The Truth, the Whole Truth, and Only *Part* of the Truth."

In this classic wholesaler *faux pas,* the advisor is told *most* of the important points about the product, leaving out only those that may make her product a little less attractive than the competition.

The charge back policy might be a classic example. Why bring it up if it's not a core strength of the product?

Because it's the *right* thing to do!

The advisor will not appreciate half a story when the issue that was not disclosed comes back to bite her. The highest possible road is the only road to take.

What about you? Are you destined for greatness or simply a pretender?

 ## Nobody Works Past 5 O'Clock

One Monday the heater in our spa went on the blink. Seemed that the flame on the gas-fed unit was not firing.

So I called the pool guy that services it and he gladly informed me that he had a "heater guy" who he'd get on the case right away.

Four days passed, so I called him again on Thursday afternoon at 4:58 PM.

Me: Did you get hold of the heater guy and when is he coming to fix it?

Pool Guy: My day was slammed, and I completely forgot to call him ... (brief pause) ... and it's 5:00. *Nobody works past 5 so I'll call him in the morning.*

Really?

Virgins Wanted

Last week I attended a dinner for financial advisors. As the first drinks were being served and the conversation was starting to rev up, I asked the advisors on either side of me the standard questions about where they worked and how long they had been in the business.

As common courtesy dictated, they asked the same questions of me and I explained my last role, before becoming a corporate expatriate, as the president of a product distributor.

As soon as they heard the name of my former firm, they both said, almost in unison, "Then you know Troy!"

Without additional prodding the rep on my left beamed and offered, "Troy is the best to ever call on me. He and I met when I was brand new, and he was the only one that took the time to explain not only what the product was, but also how to sell it."

The rep on my right added, "He helped me with the positioning of the product, where it best fit, and even how to drop a ticket on our order entry system."

Then in two-part harmony they said, "Troy's great!"

Like Troy, when I was wholesaling, many of my best clients started as virgins.

They had no experience with my product, and I had the great good fortune to be "the guy."

And you can be the guy or gal too.

The guy who showed them the whole process, soup to nuts. Sometimes that meant starting all the way at the beginning with the most basic education — such as, "What's a mutual fund?"

The gal who helped them craft the pitch. Showing them how to use the brochure, or yellow pad, and giving them the right words to say.

The guy who worked with them on the close.

Your reward?

Like the reps fondly referring to Troy many years later, you'll have clients who fondly recall their times with you and who speak in only the most glowing of terms about you.

Too frequently wholesalers don't take the time necessary to teach new advisors how to sell. They often assume that the feature and benefit discussion will allow the advisors to put all the presentation pieces together.

While part-time elephant hunting (chasing the biggest advisor game) can occasionally result in a big *kill*, your more rewarding time is frequently better spent with thoughtfully selected virgins.

TMT — The Only Thing a Wholesaler Has to Offer

In a recent discussion with a Divisional Manager coaching client, he described an activity he was doing with COIs (Centers of Influence). I questioned him as to why *he* was the one engaging in the activity that a lesser trained, less expensive staff member could do with the exact same results.

The rationale holds true for wholesalers as well.

A wholesaler's job is both complex and simple.

Not simple as in easy — far from it.

Simple as in you have three things to offer prospects and clients: time, money, and talent — TMT.

Time is your most valuable commodity. In the 2011 Wholesaler Satisfaction Survey we found that 45% of wholesalers were making over $200k per year.

Said another way, 45% of wholesalers are making over $100 per hour.

How do you spend your time?

At this hourly rate, I hope it's not doing an over abundance of "grunt" work.

If you have the ability to hire someone at $15 per hour to do that work, it frees you up to make better use of the time you have.

Money: You are blessed with an expense account. It makes the job of winning the hearts and minds of advisors that much easier.

Why is it that too many wholesalers fritter away the money without regard to how the money is used to leverage and multiply the business?

Your $50-$100k annual expense budget should be viewed as the greatest fulcrum in the world.

Don't spend unless you have at least a cursory idea of why you are spending and what you hope to gain.

Talent: You are a uniquely talented professional. Make sure that the payoff for the investment of your talent is understood before committing.

As an example, I'll assume that you do well in front of public audiences and are an in-demand speaker. If that's the case, why would you consider giving this skill away without knowing what the intended outcome would be?

Shouldn't you understand what the production target is from the rep that asks you to invest your talent in his business?

The same holds true if you are an expert in practice management, portfolio construction, client meetings, etc.

If you were running your own business, you would not make a move without understanding the TMT implications.

And the reality is you *are* running a business and you need to be thinking about TMT — every day.

Apparently, I live in a region of the country where termites are particularly fierce.

And the fact that I am just now realizing this after 30 years in Southern California is somewhat embarrassing.

Nonetheless, it was time to consider getting the house tented before I came home to find sawdust where there was once hardwood flooring.

The thing was we needed to leave the house for three days, put the pets in dog care/cat care/bird care, and make sure the house was emptied of anything that would later be eaten or touched so as not to die from termite gas.

All of this sounded like one overwhelming pain in the butt.

Being a buy-locally, think-globally kind of guy, I decided to give a local company a call rather than call the national exterminator services.

So I called and scheduled my Termite Terry complimentary 57 Point Inspection.

Upon arrival the representative from Termite Terry, whose name I don't recall, gave me a full education in termites, their destructive ways, and his master plan to eradicate them from my home.

After completion of his 57th Point, the rep did something that struck me.

He pulled out his sales war book and showed me photographs he had taken of all the bad tenting jobs his competitors had done. This included jobs where tents ended up blowing in the wind, or where tents had been placed so loosely on the home that all the termite-killing gas leaked out.

Clearly he had a future as a member of the Hollywood paparazzi.

He also spent as much time selling me on the benefits of using his company for repairing the wood damage after the tenting as he did selling the tenting job itself.

Being a good consumer, and knowing absolutely nothing about termite control, I knew getting another estimate was the right thing to do — and I called Terminex.

Larko (yes, Larko, who's from Peru and liked to drink Pisco) showed up for his inspection. Both The Mrs. and I were immediately struck by his knowledge, professionalism, and matter-of-fact confidence.

During his pitch, Larko:

- stayed myopically focused on his expertise — eliminating termites;

- answered each question with a certainty borne out of his experience and his conviction;

- made the process seem far less onerous than I had imagined and feared;

- never took a jab at a competitor; and
- deftly navigated the price discussion to a comfortable win-win.

And the clincher?

After building all that rapport and trust, he assured us that he'd be at the house to supervise the entire process.

You know I inked the deal with Larko, who happened to work for Terminex.

 ## Why Wholesaling Is Like Roofing Tiles, Only Different

Recently we had our house tented for termites — an event that I wish on no one that you know, and certainly not on you.

If you are not familiar (can we trade places?) this is where many five-foot tall men show up and swarm your roof, placing huge tarps that "wrap" the whole house in a somewhat airtight seal so that the gas, that will surely kill any and all things it comes in contact with, will stay in the wrapper.

Got the picture?

Anyway, as you might imagine: people walking on your roof = cracked roof tiles.

In my search for replacement tiles (Mission style, both field and edge, if you must know), I went to retailer #1 who insisted that the field tile was no longer made and that I would need to go to another place that reclaims tiles from old homes.

So I went.

And the salesman there pulled out the sales brochure and asked me which of eight color styles I'd like to purchase — *new*.

Are you following me?

Lesson: Never insist that something is irrefutably one way if you even have the slightest thought that you might be wrong. In this situation the salesman at retailer #1 was dead wrong, which proved to me that he — and perhaps by extension his company — didn't know their products.

Result?

I can't shop there in the future (heaven forbid) because I don't trust their expertise

The Purpose of Repurposing — From the Department of Redundancy Department

Wholesalers, repeat this mantra after me: *I will repurpose content. I will repurpose content. I will re…*

Creating content that is new and original, such as

- sales ideas
- email messages to advisors
- sales meeting presentations
- one-on-one content
- lunch meeting presentations
- walk-through snippets
- branch trainings
- agency training

takes a ton of work, especially if you are recreating each message from scratch.

That's where the repurpose mantra comes in — and it's one we need to repeat to ourselves often here at Wholesaler Masterminds as we create blog posts, newsletters, coaching sessions, podcasts and classroom coaching.

Here's an example.

You get an email from an advisor that reads:

Dear Superstar Wholesaler:

I just wanted to let you know that the sales idea you provided to me the other day worked like magic. The way you tied the story about inverse correlation of the Foonman Commodity Fund to the Foonman We're Still Solvent Small Town Muni Fund was pure genius.

I only wish every wholesaler was as freaking brilliant as you.

Can't wait for our next meeting!

Most wholesalers would file (or worse, delete) this after replying to the rep.

But, if you think to yourself, *"Hey, I'll repurpose this content,"* then you will use this same email for:

- A quick note to your boss (you are managing your career, right?) that simply reads:

    Yes, this was actually written by one of my reps — pretty great, huh?

    I'd be happy to provide this idea on our next sales call.

- A "Success Alert" blast to your Top 50 reps that says:

    There's no way I could make up this email.

    If we have not yet discussed this concept, we need to meet — soon!

The opening of your next rep meeting:

> "Since everyone here knows that I am not beyond shameless self-promotion, I wanted to share an email I received this week and then explain how the concept works."

Remind yourself to repurpose — it saves time and energy, and it works.

Gimme Pastrami on Rye

When I was a kid, my family lived in New York. As anyone who grew up in NYC knows, one of the great foods of the city is delicatessen or deli.

Now I'm not sure what your favorite deli menu item is, but my favorite is pastrami on rye with Russian dressing on the side. Some folks are mustard kind of folks, but make mine Russian dressing, and lots of it.

Recently, I had the opportunity to go to NYC on business, and one of the most important stops, besides my client, was a deli. Not just any deli though, one of the great landmark Manhattan establishments.

For a couple of weeks before my trip I was telling friends that, in the absence of great quality deli in Orange County, this had become a high priority stop.

My anticipation and expectations were high.

Having arrived in NYC at about 6:30, it was time for the moment about which I had been salivating for weeks.

On 7th Avenue, in the mid-50s and within two blocks of one another, are two of the great delicatessens in the city. Stage Deli and Carnegie Deli have been churning out phenomenal food for decades. Famous films have had their most memorable scenes filmed in the dining room of these delis — think *Broadway Danny Rose*.

I approached the Stage Deli counter, eager to place my order.

"Pastrami on rye with Russian dressing on the side, to go please," I said.

Moments later, a bag appeared on the counter.

"Russian dressing in the bag?" I confirmed with the counterman.

"Absolutely, two packets!" he assured me.

On the way back to the hotel to consume this wonderful tower of goodness I kept thinking, "He said packet; since when does a NYC deli serve Russian dressing in a packet?"

Once in my room, I unwrapped the object of my culinary desire. My eyes met a tower of pastrami on rye, with two packets of *Kraft Thousand Island* dressing.

Wait, KRAFT THOUSAND ISLAND DRESSING?! (sorry to yell)

My experience was shot. The entire meal was relegated to just another sandwich in just another city.

The experience I had expected and eagerly anticipated was now damaged beyond repair.

My guess is that using Kraft Thousand Island dressing allows Stage Deli to save money, curb waste, and deliver a more efficient "to go" process. I'd even be willing to bet that this change to Kraft packets was made recently as business slowed due to the recession.

And that's where it jumped the rails.

In pursuit of cost savings and efficiency, the very core of the product had been compromised.

Would there be brand damage if Four Seasons Hotels replaced L'Occitane toiletries with Dial?

You bet there would be.

What about your product, your business, your brand?

it's all in the details

Have the assorted economic crosswinds and the accompanying need to streamline, cost cut, and reinvent your product done harm to the very core of your perceived value in the marketplace?

Footnote to this Story: On November 30, 2012, the Stage Deli closed after 75 years in business. The owners cited the toll the recession had taken, along with spiraling rent costs, as the reason for closing according to *The New York Times*.

There was no mention in *The Time's* story about the impact of Kraft Thousand Island Dressing packets.

How to Craft a Story and Spin it

When you are a student of the business, you are able to emit knowledge about our industry and your sector that really gives the client great confidence that you know a lot about your subject matter. In fact, it infers an education level that you may not even have.

Some wholesalers can pick up the morning paper, read a headline or two, and run the entire day with a great story to tell every rep they touch.

Some wholesalers need help. Here's a six-step process that you can follow for spinning a great story from today's headlines.

Note: We have transcribed the original 2010 video located at the Wholesaler Masterminds website to offer you the following step-by-step process.

The Wall Street Journal weekend edition's headlines and a few well chosen paragraphs allow us to construct the compelling story. The first headline says, "Economy Is Still Bleeding Jobs." This comes off the Friday job report where 85,000 jobs were unexpectedly lost. This comes on the heels of a November report where there was actually a small uptick in the number of jobs created. Now you would have thought on the surface that the market would have tanked based upon that particular story.

Step 1 was to read the business page, and Step 2 was to pick out the hot story of the day. The hot story of this day was the jobs report.

What does it mean to the economy? This is Step 3. On the surface, you'd think that what it means to the economy is that there is not as much growth as otherwise expected.

The second headline was found in the second section of *The Journal*. It said that stocks ended higher the first week of 2010. As a matter of fact, reading only the first and second paragraphs of the story, because I know how pressed for time you are, I learned that Ned Davis Research tells us that from 1900 to 2006 the average increase in the first week of January is 0.6%, and the first week of January 2010 it was an increase of 1.8%.

So why didn't the market tank on Friday? Well, the market didn't tank on Friday because the market believes overall there is growth on the horizon.

What does it mean to the investor? That's Step 4.

To the investor it very well might mean that all is not lost when it comes to equity gains. In fact, 2009 was a fabulous recovery year. 2010 might well be a year where we add onto some of those gains, although not as graciously. It also means to the investor that at the back end of 2010 we might actually start to see an increase in interest rates.

Step 5: What does it mean to the advisor? If you are a wholesaler talking to a financial advisor, what does it mean to them?

What it means to them is they've got to think long and hard about continuing to sell only short-term bond funds. So many advisors have been selling so many billions of dollars in short-term bond funds and the worm will turn and rates will rise and interest sensitive funds will go down in value.

What does it mean to the advisor? It means they need to start diversifying their sales. If the client insists on something safe and secure, maybe 75% should be allocated into a short-term bond fund and 25% goes into a balance fund or into a fund that specializes in rising dividends. As the economy continues to repair, dividends should increase.

Step 6 is how can I, my product or my firm help the investor?

Mr. Advisor, we have two funds that I think would be of interest to you. Number one is the short-term bond fund you've been selling. Number two is our utilities fund, which has a history dating back to 1955 and an average annual return, even considering 2009, of 7.7% since inception. I think if you do a one-two punch here next time you see the client, you'll be able to start to hedge your bets.

Practice how to become better at spinning a story with the six-step process:

1. Read the business page. Or if you set up Google Reader you can preset your RSS feeds and all those stories will come to you to spin your story for the day.

2. What's the hot story?

3. What does it mean for the economy?

4. What does it mean for investors?

5. What does it mean to the advisor?

6. How can my firm, my product, or I help?

One element of being a great student of the business is how you can craft these stories to give a brilliant spin on all the information you want to be able to convey to the advisor, the client, the prospect.

In doing this, you absolutely, positively rise out of the Sea of Sameness and you increase your MQ — Memorability Quotient® along the way.

Do You Give Good Phone?

How well do you use voice mail?

A lot of clients that I've been talking to recently find themselves ridiculously pressed for time. Perhaps even more than normal for a wholesaler.

Maybe it has something (everything?) to do with the economy improving.

They lament that they'd like to be able to reach more advisors and they feel compelled to want to reach these advisors live via phone. And, because they would like to reach them in person, they plan to do the dialing during regular business hours.

Then they get busy and don't call. Sound familiar?

I often suggest to these clients that they should get better at using voice mail.

Now this may sound obvious to you, but a lot of wholesalers who feel like they must reach the client live are overlooking the fact that just leaving the message is letting the advisor *feel the love*.

Use voice mail messages to:

- Let the advisor know that you reached out to follow up on the hypothetical illustration that was sent earlier in the day.

- Let the advisor know that you've followed up on a literature fulfillment order that went out last week.
- Let the advisor know that you appreciate that last ticket that was written.

All of these can be done efficiently through the use of voice mail.

As a matter of fact, what I suggest you do is use voice mail during the hours when you know positively that the phone number you have dialed will roll to voice mail, that is, at 6:00 in the morning or at 8:00 at night.

You can hit 10, 20, 30 different people in the course of one session, spread lots of love, and at the same time not have to get bogged down in a conversation that may take up to 3, 5, 10 minutes.

Now granted, there will be certain circumstances where you don't get the power of the same touch that you have with a live conversation, and this tactic is not designed to replace all direct contacts. Yet more times than not it's simply the act of the advisor hearing your voice that gets the message through that you're on top of your business, following up and staying connected.

And what does that mean?

You increase your MQ — Memorability Quotient®.

So, do you give good phone?

How to Butcher a Prospect

My Dad is 83.

At this point in his life he is making sure that his financial house is in order, both for his future and for the future of his family.

And he needs a financial advisor to assist him.

While I am licensed, frankly I am not capable — it would be like practicing medicine on your family member.

I was referred to an advisor near my Dad's home and I called.

Me: "May I speak to Peter, please?"

Receptionist: "He's away from his desk. Can he call you right back?"

Peter returned the call … *four days later.*

In the meantime, I got ticked off because where I come from "away from his desk" doesn't translate into calling back four days later.

It turns out that Peter was not away from his desk — he was on personal time off.

And so began an unnecessarily rocky start to what might be a great prospect for the advisor.

Making sure your message is delivered in the right manner seems so simple doesn't it?

Too bad it's just not that easy.

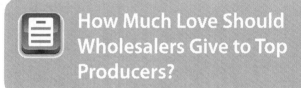

How Much Love Should Wholesalers Give to Top Producers?

I had a boss who always used to say, "Your best clients are your competitor's best prospects."

And that means you need to guard the relationship you have with your top producers — closely.

That said, have you ever wondered how much is too much when catering to the needs of your very best clients?

Is it possible to love your top producers too much?

How do you draw the line between relationship building and pandering?

Great wholesalers are mindful of this line and are able to navigate the subtleties.

The "right" advisor relationships are built on partnerships, not an awkward sense of servitude that gets compounded by the producer's ability to drop tickets and the wholesaler's need to exceed their production/income goals.

Every wholesaler I know has been at the crossroads of the "whale" who can/does put up huge numbers but is also a slime bag.

These are the reps who have the gall to demand outrageous sums of marketing support (often even before a trade is done), expect (versus graciously accept) invitations to high profile events, and even have a tendency to be abusive to home office partners.

Years ago I began to call this the "seamy underbelly" of our business, and, based on my conversations with wholesalers every day, that underbelly is still very much alive and well.

In a recent email to our subscribers I wrote about a due diligence attendee I was entertaining who, after drinking way too much, started belligerently mouthing off to strangers on the streets of Manhattan.

Was his $2 million a year in production worth it to me?

Have you compromised any of your beliefs or personal ethics in pursuit of the "right" relationships with huge producers?

 ## 8 Ounces of Water Worth $5,000?

Vacation season is upon us.

And The Mrs. and I are just back from the wine country where we tend to gravitate to — a lot.

On one of our trips some five years ago, we drove to a then newer resort tucked up in the north end of Napa Valley — in the town of Calistoga.

As we approached the resort, simply to have a look for future reference, we were told by the exceedingly polite valet that the resort was only open to guests.

Then with a large smile on his face, he asked, "Would you like an ice cold bottle of water for the rest of your journey?"

Are you getting this?

We were looky-loos driving an average enough rental car.

He could have easily dismissed us as riffraff and sent us packing.

But he didn't.

Since that day, my wife has remembered that 8-oz. act of kindness.

This past week it resulted in over $5,000 in revenue for the resort, as we had a fine time celebrating our wedding anniversary at Calistoga Ranch.

Reminders for us all: Never judge a book by its looky-loo cover — and the simplest acts can pay the largest dividends.

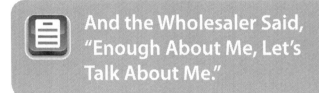

And the Wholesaler Said, "Enough About Me, Let's Talk About Me."

At a two-hour workshop for a group of wholesalers, we completed an activity to strengthen the quality of the questions they asked both existing advisors (to deepen the relationship) and prospects (to find the point of pain).

As the group was sharing which of the "76 Great Questions Wholesalers Should Ask Advisors" (see later in this section) they would be adding to their repertoire, one wholesaler piped in.

"Rob, I've been a wholesaler since 1993 and in all that time I have found that my best approach in appointments is to talk about me. Reps want to know about my accomplishments, why I'm qualified, and what I can bring to the equation," he said.

He continued, "If I'm the sixth guy in his office that asks him the same questions he's just going to get aggravated."

My reply was, "I respectfully disagree."

Now I'd like to amend that answer. "I couldn't disagree more."

When was the last time you were successfully sold anything by someone who only talked about themselves?

Isn't the whole point of asking *great* questions (not to be confused with the standard, seemingly obligatory, BS questions) and then *listening to the answers with a high degree of empathy* to get insights that help you formulate how you'll sell to the prospect?

To demonstrate your ability to walk in the advisor's shoes?

To find out where their pain is?

To discern what solutions you'll provide that will be attractive?

The whole exchange of questions and answers is about client discovery, yes?

And it's also about the foundational building blocks of solid advisor relationships that are formed by what you ask and how you react/respond.

What questions are you asking your advisors? How well are you listening?

The Allure of the Filler Appointment

The demands on a wholesaler are great.

Both from the advisors they serve and the managers who employ them.

One of those demands is activity.

Most firms have requirements that say a wholesaler should see 12 (low end) to 20 advisors during the course of the week.

In pursuit of those numbers — especially on the more aggressive end of the activity spectrum — we find wholesalers who spend too much time with The Filler.

Not unlike an award ceremony where The Filler is called upon to occupy a bona fide star's seat while the star is fixing their makeup in the bathroom, The Filler advisor serves but one purpose.

To pad your activity count so you can make the "quota."

Sadly, that means that you're wasting time with The Filler — who has no intention of writing (and a proven history of doing no more than $50k) with you in the course of the year — when you could be converting Dabblers or seeing Game Changers.

So, tempting though it may be, you need to stop The Filler appointments — because you're not winning any awards by seeing them.

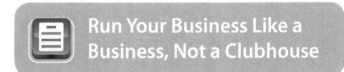

Denver: lunch with Gail.

Boise: cocktails with Lou.

Salt Lake City: dinner with Al.

Next rotation = lather, rinse, repeat.

I have a wholesaler coaching client who is really tight with most of his reps. And you'd expect him to be since he has spent more than five years in a small geographic territory.

The problem is his appointments have turned into social visits.

He was running a mobile clubhouse. Yes, there were lots of collegial conversations, great stories, and big laughs. Hell, it was a love-fest.

The problem was that the same advisors who were in his clubhouse weren't writing any business.

And that got the boss's attention — fast.

Now the same wholesaler runs his territory like a business. Yes, he still has great friends in the region; he just doesn't see the great friends that aren't writing his business during office hours.

He closed the clubhouse.

And as a result of this, and other great work on his part, he's been over his monthly goal for the last four months.

How about you? Are you running a business or a clubhouse?

Do You Get Dirty in Your Territory's Data?

When you look at your territory, do you get dirty in the data?

What I mean by that is, do you take the opportunity to parse all of the different data points that are available to set up your rotations and zones effectively?

So many wholesalers I talk to are still running by the seat of their pants in their territories. And when they sit down to actually put zones and rotations together, they find themselves at a loss for exactly what types of data they should be looking at.

In a recent discussion with one of my Wholesaler Masterminds coaching clients, I was speaking with them about those different data points and which to use to construct the best and most potentially profitable rotations.

For this particular wholesaler it was first looking at the Barron's Top 1,000 List to match that list against sellers and prospects in his territory, as he is in an area of the country well represented by these advisors.

Next, he needed to look at the Market Metrics data to understand where the producers were, in what offices, in what cities.

Finally, he looked at the "fallen angel" list — those producers who had not done business over the course of the last year, but had done business, say, in the year prior. He layered those in.

He added in the current top 100 sellers in the territory.

And tossed in the region's top 25 prospects.

From there, he needed to go through and carefully map out which firms, from those lists, had advisors in the densest concentration in the various cities in his territory.

Only then did it become clear(er) where he should be spending his most valuable time to maximize his opportunity.

Now, rest assured, none of this is easy lifting. As a matter of fact, it's very heavy lifting.

But, in order to construct the right zones and rotations in your region, you need to get dirty in the data.

So, do you get dirty?

 Simple, Not Easy

DeeAnne was a wholesaler in Northern California.

On a ride-a-long with her, we stopped off at Fred's office who was the 1,100 lb. producer at his broker/dealer.

DeeAnne explained to me that Fred only gave her ten minutes so she was closing for another, longer appointment.

Frankly I couldn't tell if the meeting was successful — but who can tell in ten minutes?

Later that week Fred called DeeAnne for help on a large ticket.

She called back promptly.

Fred dropped a $600,000 ticket.

Later, DeeAnne learned from Fred that on that day he called five wholesalers for help — one right after another.

Two have still yet to return his call — and this was more than eight years ago.

Two thought that 24 hours was good enough response time.

One — that would be DeeAnne — jumped on the call.

You see, operating with a high degree of urgency is simple, but not easy.

If urgency was important to 1,100 lb. gorilla Fred eight years ago, how much more important is it today in a world of hyper-connected advisors?

76 Great Questions Wholesalers Should Ask Advisors

If I've said it once, I've said it 100 times: "Wholesalers who partner with advisors (AEs, agents, reps, etc.) are a valuable commodity."

Those who show up and throw up are a dime a dozen.

Where do you fit in?

In order to assist you with becoming a consultative business partner to advisors and elevate you out of the sea of wholesaler sameness, check out the questions below.

1. How long have you been in financial services sales (broker, agent, RIA, etc.)?
2. What licenses do you hold?
3. Where did you go to school?
4. Tell me about your staff.
5. What does each team member do?
6. What's your money management process?
7. How are product decisions made?
8. Are there specific models that you follow?
9. Do you use formal product screening processes?
10. What is your asset allocation model today?

11. How will that change over the next three years?

✓ 12. Do you perform full financial plans for all clients? If not, is there a threshold?

13. What programs do you use to generate the financial plan?

✓ 14. Can I get a copy of your client fact finder?

15. How do you engage the client's attorney?

16. How do engage the client's CPA?

17. How many attorneys and CPAs do you partner with?

✓ 18. Tell me about your client ranking process. Do you use revenues, households, dollars over or under certain thresholds, or A-B-C-D ranking?

✓ 19. What are your total assets under management?

20. What's your average account size?

✓ 21. How many clients do you have in total?

22. When was the last time you pruned your book?

23. Explain to me what you did to grow revenue last year.

✓ 24. How successful are you at obtaining client referrals?

✓ 25. What percentage of your book has been generated from client referral?

✓ 26. What was the last program, class, or presentation you attended for professional development?

✓ 27. How successfully do you feel you are managing your team? Where could you use assistance?

28. What wholesalers provide you with the most support and/or value? Why?

29. What was your product mix last year?

30. How will that change in the year ahead?

√ 31. How are you reaching out to the next generation of your clients (i.e., children, grandchildren)?

√ 32. Why do clients like doing business with you?

33. Explain to me your PVP — Peerless Value Proposition®.

√34. Tell me about your client communication strategy (i.e., frequency, communication channels).

35. May I have a copy of your latest client communication (newsletter, blast email, etc.)?

36. Who's your toughest competitor? Why?

37. Is there a new product or asset class that you're exploring for your client portfolios?

38. Do you work with business assets?

39. Do you work with company retirement plans?

40. Tell me about the product mix of your book (funds, annuities, ETFs, insurance).

√41. Who is/was your mentor in business?

√ 42. What was the greatest lesson you learned from them?

√ 43. Tell me about your family.

√44. If you could change one thing about your practice this year what would it be?

√45. What's the hardest part of your job?

46. What do you like the most about being a financial advisor?

47. How do you decompress from the demands of the job?

48. How did you fare in 2008-2009?

49. What would you have done differently during the meltdown?

✓ 50. What was your greatest lesson from the Great Recession?

✓ 51. Can you share your five-year targets for your practice (revenue, assets, income, staff size)?

52. What accreditations do you have?

53. What local business, social, or charity organizations do you belong to?

✓ 54. What keeps you up at night?

✓ 55. What is the biggest impediment to taking your production to the next level?

56. Can you share with me your formal marketing plan?

57. Have you ever engaged the services of a coach? If so, what areas of focus were most successful for you?

58. What are your favorite business publications to read?

✓ 59. Tell me the title of the last book you read.

60. What's your favorite travel destination?

61. What are your thoughts on our industry looking out five years?

62. What's been the most successful client acquisition strategy you have used?

63. Have you ever used virtual assistance (e.g., elance, guru, Hire My Mom)?

64. What conferences do you normally attend for continuing education/peer interaction?

65. Have you ever belonged to an advisor mastermind group?

66. How has technology assisted your business?

67. Where do you need help with technology?

68. Do you use RSS (i.e., Google Reader) to stay abreast of your clients, prospects, and news?

69. What CRM do you use?

70. What is your favorite part of being a financial advisor?

71. Where do you feel that you/your team really excel versus the competition?

72. How do you describe your practice to new prospects? What's your elevator speech?

73. What are the most important criteria to you when considering a new product provider/wholesaler relationship?

74. How can I best assist you in meeting your goals?

75. How do you engage in new media/social media — including blogging, LinkedIn, Facebook, Twitter?

76. To date, what's the #1 lesson you've learned in your business?

Use these questions to demonstrate your profiling prowess and separate yourself from the wholesaling Sea of Sameness.

10 Ways Wholesalers Can Increase Their Likeability

Go out to Google right now and search for "People do business with people that they like" and then stand back. You'll find almost 1.5 million results, and there is a broad range of opinions on both sides of the argument.

Here's what I know to be true: I can't name one wholesaler who is at the top of her game who got there by being unlikeable. Loveable? Perhaps not. Likeable? Absolutely.

So what are the traits that make for a most likeable wholesaler? If you were to hold a mirror up to the following attributes, how would you fare?

1. **Empathetic:** Being empathetic allows you to live for a moment in the shoes of the client and their practice. It means that you take the time to develop an understanding for the inner working of the advisor's business so you may determine how to best serve them. It also means that you are attuned to their personal travails as the relationship deepens.

2. **Responsive:** How many business relationships do you let into your life that are run by unresponsive people? My guess is not many. In fact, I'll bet that you have parted company with a vendor or service provider when they have failed to meet your standard of responsiveness. With all the choices available to the

advisor, why should they be any different? In a hyper-connected world, the notion of even 24-hour turnaround for returning calls seems to fall short.

3. **Advocative:** People who have your back are people who people like. Are you an advocate for your clients when it comes to fighting the good fight, say on a home office decision that didn't go in the advisor's favor even though the case appeared strongly in their favor?

4. **Chameleon-like:** One of the all-time requirements for great wholesalers is the ability to form relation-ships with a wide range of advisors. This includes your ability to form a working relationship even with those folks who, frankly, you don't like. No, you don't have an obligation to put up with abusive clients, but finding common business ground with the broadest array of sellers can only inure your value to them, which will benefit you.

5. **Well-mannered:** One client of ours stresses the importance of the seemingly simple act of being a gentleman/woman. He told me about the all too often overlooked notion of treating others as you wish to be treated. When I grew up my parents used to remind me to "mind my p's and q's." While there are different theories on the origin of the expression, the one that connects to our business suggests that it was borne out of English pub owners reminding clients to watch their alcohol consumption — to mind their pints and quarts.

6. **Vulnerable:** The notion of vulnerability evokes different meaning for different wholesalers. To some it's an unthinkable characteristic because it can be associated with weakness. Conversely, great wholesalers know that letting their superman/woman guard down just enough to show their more human side has powerfully alluring qualities to many prospects and clients.

Here are three examples of vulnerability in action.

- Your ability to say, "I don't know. I'll need to get back to you with an answer."

- Having selectively personal discussions with reps about challenges or obstacles — with "selectively" being the operative word.

- Allowing advisors to learn more about you via a social media channel that has more personal interaction (rather than solely business interactions), i.e., Facebook.

7. **Optimistic:** Who doesn't get dragged down by the endless pessimist? Those influences in our lives that constantly find only the negative and are rarely willing to find the positive are vampires that suck the life out of us. Why then should we expect our clients to develop an affinity for us if pessimism is our MO? In that 30-60-minute window of time that you have to spend with an advisor, do your best to be the bright spot in their day — they have enough of their own issues without living in yours.

8. **Straight-shooter**: How's your BS detector? Chances are your reps have as finely tuned a BS detection devise as you do. Then why is it that so many wholesalers insist on bluffing, dancing, or cajoling their way through a tough situation when the simple act of shooting straight is so much more effective and attractive?

9. **Dependable:** If we have said it once, we have said it a million times, "Do what you say you're going to do, when you say you're going to do it." This may sound easy to do while you read it here, but it is actually far less easy to achieve in day-to-day business. The good news is that you have the ability to control both sides of the statement. You can make decisions about what you commit to do *and* you have complete control over when you have committed to making it happen.

10. **Humble:** Part of the DNA of all great wholesalers has to do with their egos. However, some wholesalers have a DNA strand that is misaligned. They are compelled to place themselves before all others, to sing (shout?) their own praises, and to generally bore others with their own self-aggrandizement. Quiet humility and the supreme confidence of knowing your own success will always lead others to you.

How likeable are you?
How wide of a likeability net do you cast?

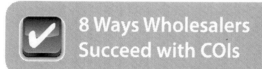
While preparing a story for *I Carry The Bag … the official magazine of wholesaling*, we interviewed COIs (Centers of Influence) in all channels.

The scope of our learning was broad.

Here are a few tidbits (8 of more than 30) that we took away from a Merrill Lynch Complex Manager.

1. Be respectful of time.

"I almost never talk to wholesalers who have not scheduled time to speak. However, those who call ahead and want to schedule 10 minutes, I almost never say no to."

He also emphasized that for him 10 minutes was the magic number.

Not 15 minutes. Not a half an hour.

2. Use schedulers wisely.

Calls that come to him for a meeting, if placed by a scheduler and are the first meeting, will almost never get calendared.

"To me it feels like a generic and random cold call. The first call should come from the wholesaler themselves."

✓ 3. I don't want a commercial for all of your products.

"Pick two best ideas. Two that I should remember and pass along."

4. Know you are "on the clock."

"Time I spend with a wholesaler is a time debit. As a result, give me something selfless — and get to the point quickly."

For this COI a perfect meeting is:

- three minutes: Rapport building
- three minutes: Ideas to make my life easier (or more profitable) as a manager
- three minutes: On your product

5. It's not about you.

Be selfless, and that means sharing the resources that wholesalers have at their disposal.

This might be from their firm and/or it might be sharing what works at the complex up the street.

6. Stay original and fresh.

With great wholesalers you can't tell the size of their territory.

That means that they are not sitting down and spewing a canned story that they have repeated 100 times.

7. **Operate like an insider.**

   The best wholesalers know the terminology of our shop.

   "During our integration with Bank of America we actually had wholesalers who helped us navigate the acronyms and helped us map the BOA to Merrill acronyms."

8. **Find alternatives.**

   Know that there are other resources besides the manager who can be just as valuable.

   Some managers will not meet with wholesalers, period.

   How are your COI relationships?

8 Ways Wholesalers Can Improve Their Presentation Skills

Recently, I attended an event that afforded me an opportunity to hear seven 30-minute wholesaler presentations, back to back.

The presenters ranged from seasoned and long-tenured professionals to a couple of newer folks.

These presentations reminded me of some tips that the best speakers practice — and rest assured that the best speakers do practice often.

1. **Plan your opening:** The very first words that you speak to the audience should be something other than:

   - "Is this on?" (referring to the microphone)
   - "How's everybody doing today?"
   - "Well, I'll make this brief because after the next speaker you get lunch."

   Instead, try opening with one of the following:

   - A story that grabs the audience's attention
   - A bold statement
   - A compelling quote

2. **Watch where you stand:** Even the most seasoned presenters can get lost on stage. Take an extra minute before you are introduced to get a sense of where you should stand.

   More than once, I saw a wholesaler position themselves between attendee tables, such that their back was to two audience members for the majority of their talk.

✓3. **Be mindful of data dumps:** Our business is filled with data. Tons and tons of it.

   Yet your audience doesn't have the capacity to digest more than small bites of spoken data points.

   Avoid statements like, "The Foonman Funds has been in business since December 3rd of 1952, with offices in 200 cities, supporting over 13,000 employees. We pride ourselves on the fact that all of our 300 funds are in the top 10% of their Lipper peer group, which is a testament to the 600 investment professionals who provide this stellar performance to over 130,000 advisors."

   Think I'm exaggerating?

   This same data hurling occurs when wholesalers are compelled to spew performance data for YTD, one-year, five-year, ten-year and life-of-fund periods of time.

4. **Match your allotted time with your slides:** You only have 30 minutes, but the firm has outfitted you with

150 slides in the "Building Bridges to a Brighter Retirement Tomorrow" presentation?

Don't flip through the first 30 while standing on stage to get to the place where you want to start the talk.

5. **Beware of audience polling overload:** An occasional question to poll the audience can be a valuable tool.

   But 10 such questions in 30 minutes will simply result in the audience refusing to play the polling game.

6. **Don't decide for the audience how they'll feel about your talk/topic:** There's a big difference between self-sabotage and self-deprecation.

   When you mention the fact that the material you are going to speak about is dry, boring, tedious, old, tired, worn, or otherwise rife to be ignored, guess what?

   You are going to be tuned out!

7. **Know your material, please:** It just isn't acceptable for you to stand at the front of the room and read an entire slide.

   And it's even less acceptable for you to do so with your back to the audience.

8. **We can't know it's the 300th time you've given this presentation:** Heaven knows that part of the wholesaler's job is to give the same presentation countless times.

And great wholesalers never let that fact appear to be so.

If you are bored with the content, if you are tired of repeating it, your audience will know!

Special message for all the marketing departments: Often wholesalers are sent out into the field with PowerPoint presentations that contain slides that have more words or graphs or charts on them than the human eye can possibly see from 50 feet (500 feet?) away: *Please Stop!!!*

Yes, we are in an industry that requires disclosures, I get that.

We are not, however, in an industry that requires you to design a slide the same way that you would a page in a brochure. And when you insist on doing this it makes your wholesalers look bad — and that's a damn shame.

Great wholesalers have great presentation skills —
how will you seek to improve yours?

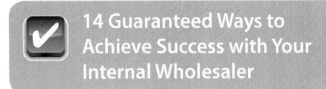

14 Guaranteed Ways to Achieve Success with Your Internal Wholesaler

Most wholesalers have an Internal Wholesaler (IW) who has become a vital piece of the business process and overall success of the region.

Sadly, from what I have seen over the years, there are wholesalers who just don't understand how to leverage these valuable folks to maximize the success of the region.

It is for you that I offer this partial list of ways to get more out of your IW and develop a great relationship.

1. Give your IW a part of the business plan to complete. At the very least, complete sections as a team.

2. Visit them in person at the home office ASAP. Nothing helps solidify a relationship faster than a face-to-face visit, an adult beverage, and a meal. Then, get together in the territory (preferred) or at the home office once per quarter.

3. Find out what your IW's careers goals are. Then explain to him how you intend to help him reach those goals. Be a mentor. When in the territory have the IW make the presentation — assuming one of his goals is to become an external wholesaler. Here's a question for you: How many of your former internals

are now external wholesalers? Managers? National Sales Managers? Made a million dollars wholesaling?

4. Set up calls once per week that are devoted to discussing only the territory. These calls should cover both strategic and tactical issues. These calls will cover more ground than the calls that the external makes into the desk as they race around throughout the day.

5. Do *not* have her do administrative work to the extent you can avoid it. Most IWs are too talented and $50-$100k is far too much money for the firm to spend in that manner.

6. Unless your firm clearly expects this of IWs, do not make him your scheduler. Go hire a scheduler if you are not doing it yourself.

7. Carve out a part of the territory that they should own and cultivate. For example, give them all your "C" advisors. Then give the IW a production goal for this group with an incentive to perform.

8. Find out what personal goals your IW aspires to. Graduate degree? Having a family? Looking for love in all the wrong places? You work too closely with this person to talk shop all the time.

9. Give your IW a piece of the budget. My IW used to have the budget for trinkets and trash. Doing so will demonstrate your trust in them and build their accountability more quickly.

10. Coordinate all the product stories and sales ideas so that you are delivering a consistent message. Record your product pitches for them. This can be done as easily as using the firm's voice mail system and laying down the tracks for the most important product pitches and sales ideas.

11. Hold your IW accountable for her part of the business plan, for her piece of the budget, for hitting her nut in production.

12. Help get your IW promoted to wherever in the firm he or she wants to go. Marketing, Portfolio Management, Wholesaling; it doesn't matter.

13. Treat your IW as a valued business partner with all of the courtesy and respect that is appropriate.

14. Take a sincere interest in their personal/non-work life. No one wants to talk business all the time — even the highest type-A wholesaler. Show a genuine interest in his life outside of the office.

Having a great partnership with your internal is one of the keys to having a Career Year.

Those who follow these suggestions are already reaping the benefits of great personal and professional success.

Great wholesalers have great relationships with their Internal Wholesalers. How successfully are you building that relationship?

@ Sometimes I'm Not Too Bright

When I covered Southern California, being stuck in traffic was a regular occurrence.

And like any time I was in the car, I was on the phone.

With advisors, COIs, prospects, and, of course, my Internal Wholesaler.

One particular internal and I had a great, albeit sometimes cantankerous, relationship and we raised a boat load of money.

One day I was giving him direction on a task that needed to be completed for the region.

He saw the outcome differently than I did.

We began to argue like a salty old married couple.

And then I threw out the, "Just f*@%ing do it — it's MY territory!"

Oh, boy, talk about the wrong thing to say.

We spent the next ten minutes arguing about who owned the territory.

What a dummy I was.

If he cared enough to fight about who owned the territory, wasn't that a *good* thing?

5 Things to Not Do at Your Next Conference

At a recent Schwab IMPACT conference, I met a cadre of unbelievable wholesaling professionals. Yet there were more than a few folks who really had a thing or two to learn about great wholesaling at a conference.

Here's list of five things to *not* do in your booth at your next conference.

1. **Read the paper at the booth:** This was not even subtle. In some cases, folks had *The Wall Street Journal* spread out like they were at the local diner eating breakfast.

2. **Talk on the phone:** Yes, you have clients to call. Yes, you have family to call. No, those calls don't need to be made from the exhibition booth.

3. **Eating meals:** Sure, we all get hungry and you need to keep your energy up for a huge show like this. That said, munching down a sub sandwich while in the booth is just plain bad form.

4. **Holding court:** These were the wholesalers who simply sat behind the six-foot table. They figured that if advisors wanted to chat they would "approach the bench" I guess.

5. **Social butterflies:** Wholesalers who spent their time doing nothing other than talking among themselves, both at their booth and others', versus talking to the participants, the Schwab advisors.

But the *coup de grâce* was the young wholesaler who sat reclined in his chair, with his feet up on the display table, talking on the phone — right under the logo of his firm's banner.

Please!

9 What Ifs: A Wholesaler's Approach to Working Conferences

Speaking of wholesalers and their effectiveness at advisor conferences, recently, it has us asking what if?

1. *What if* you worked your booth like a political candidate working a room full of moms and babies?

2. *What if* at your next conference you attended more speaking sessions/attendee events than you skipped?

3. *What if* you sought out your best clients or prospects and intentionally planted yourself next to them at one of those sessions?

4. *What if* that session together gave you an additional piece of "connective tissue" that helped solidify the advisor relationship — at the conference and at their office, which you undoubtedly will get access to visit?

5. *What if* you had a synopsis of your thoughts and observations about the conference to share with your clients and prospects via email after the event was over?

6. *What if* you committed yourself to avoiding the over indulgence that often accompanies three days of conference attendance?

7. *What if* you relentlessly followed up on that stack of business cards/leads that the conference produced?

8. *What if* conference "duty" was a gift and not a burden?

9. *What if* the $20,000 to $100,000 that your firm spent on the fee to be at the conference yielded a measurable ROI that defended the reason that the firm is even there?

What if?

 ## Brief and Occasional Train Noise

Shortcomings.

We all have them.

And sometimes we choose, unwisely, to overlook them in others.

Recently The Mrs. and I took a journey up to the Pacific Northwest and booked a hotel that had great reviews, was right on the water, and had a spa.

And it was right on the train tracks.

Prior to booking the trip, the following exchange took place with my wife.

Me: "Looks like the nicest place in town for us to stay is right on the train tracks."

Wife: "That's OK with me. I like trains — you know how they put me to sleep."

Upon check-in there was a small plaque tucked over to the right side of the registration desk that said, "Brief and Occasional Train Noise."

I said to the front desk clerk, "Wow, you are really close to the tracks!"

To which she replied, "No problem, we have ear plugs in the room."

Uh, oh.

At 3 AM, a freight train rolled through.

Judging by its size, I am fairly certain that the train had most of what the city of Vancouver, BC, needed for the next month contained in its endless stream of cars.

After that train, this is the exchange that took place.

Me: "You awake?"

Wife: "I guess trains only put me to sleep when I'm riding on them …"

And so it continued. For all four days we were there.

These are the lessons I learned:

1. Other good components of the business (spa, décor, view) can't make up for fundamental flaws.

2. You can't put lipstick on a pig. The staff at the hotel can't downplay the noise created by five trains per night.

3. Customers might try you once (as we did), but those fundamental flaws will damage your chance for a loyal, lasting tribe of followers and raving fans.

Part Two

INCREASING YOUR MQ — MEMORABILITY QUOTIENT®

 Deciding Between 4½ and 4½

I'm no spring chicken.

Not quite over the hill mind you, but old enough to be able to reflect on things that you may not have seen, heard, or thought about.

Take bank interest rates … stay with me here.

Before 1983 every bank had the same rate on the same type of account.

In fact the ad collage is from *The New York Times* on May 7, 1960.

Everyone was paying 4½% for bank deposits. So how did any one institution stand out from the pack and avoid this Sea of Sameness?

To one bank it was the "save by mail" service. To another it was the allure of stashing your money in California.

As for me, I'd want the three-piece Silverplate Salad Set.

So what does this have to do with wholesaling today?

Everything!!!

> Precious few wholesalers have anything truly unique, product-wise, in their bag.
>
> That means you need to strengthen your memorability muscle — the characteristics, attributes, talents, or processes that allow you to break out of the 4½% pack.

As the preparation for the National Sales Conference began, I was asked by the meeting planner how much time I wanted to present my keynote speech. As the newly appointed President of the distribution company I knew I needed to deliver some of the foundational thoughts that underscore my beliefs about success in our business.

One of my main points, and a pivotal part of the success of the team that I managed prior to getting my promotion, was the notion of honing the MQ — Memorability Quotient® of the team. That means figuring out how you will stay out of the vast Sea of Sameness that pervades our business.

A few years later, and now in my private coaching practice, I have developed for my clients the concept of PVP — Peerless Value Proposition® to assist them with further clarifying the importance of distinguishing themselves from every other suit, carrying every other briefcase in every other brokerage office.

So how will you avoid the nauseating, violently rough waters of the Sea of Sameness?

What's your MQ?

@ Legends and Four-Legged Friends

Next time I'm in Chattanooga, Tennessee, I need to pay closer attention.

It seems that a legend lives there.

Luther Masingill is a DJ in town, and he's been on the air at the same radio station for 72 years.

A world record.

But that's not the only thing that makes him legendary.

It's the fact that for all of those years he's been announcing lost and found pets on the radio.

He's reunited literally thousands of distraught owners with their four-legged best friends.

And in doing so he's built a reputation and following that no other radio personality in the state can claim.

What about your wholesaling practice?

Your reputation?

How will you be remembered?

What Side of the Bed Do You Sleep on?

Been thinking lately, always a dicey disclaimer, that there might well be something of a Position Paradox in the labor force.

The industry that I have called home for the last 30 years is financial services. In turn, most of the readership of my Sunday Night Email makes their living in the same field. Relative to many other industries ours is one that frequently affords us the opportunity to earn significant incomes, travel at the higher end of the five-star scale, and entertain at some of the best establishments in the country, sometimes the world.

By way of contrast, many of the employees who work at these establishments we are fortunate enough to visit can only dream of the luxuries that we often enjoy.

What's the point?

In my keynote address about Increasing Your MQ — Memorability Quotient®, I review clues to create maximum memorability.

One of these clues is *enthusiasm*.

The story that I tell to illustrate this clue has changed as a direct result of the single most enthusiastic person I have met in quite some time.

After an uneventful flight to Dallas and a quick cab ride, I arrived at the Ritz Carlton. After checking in, I headed to my room and noticed that the door to the room was ajar. I opened the door.

And a big gregarious voice, in a deep Texas accent, said, "Well hello! I'm turnin' down your room. Is that OK?" She absolutely beamed.

Now, perhaps like you, I am not used to much of a greeting from the housekeeping team other than a polite good morning every now and again.

"What side of the bed do you sleep on?" she asked with a sincere smile.

Kind of a personal question, but I'm going with it. After some brief thought and a quick calculation of the phone-to-alarm-clock-to-light-reach ratios, I pointed to the left side of the bed.

"Then that's where I'll put your water, and your chocolates and the weather report card for tomorrow."

She went on to point out some of the amenities of the room, ask me how long I would be staying, and assure me that I would be back again and again because of the friend-liness of the staff.

She then gave me a final report that her work was complete.

"I went ahead and turned down both sides of the bed in case you decide to bring home a lady friend," she smiled.

Now let me state for the record that I have been happily married for over 20 years.

"There will be none of that," I replied, and I asked what her name was.

"Anita is my name, and I hope you have a wonderful stay. If you need anything, do not hesitate to call," she said as she made her way out the door.

I was standing there with a huge grin on my face. Anita, through her *enthusiasm*, had completely transformed an otherwise unremarkable situation into one that had *Maximum Memorability* written all over it.

The Position Paradox is simply this: all of the money and perks of the industry we call home will do nothing to increase our MQ. In fact, some of the people who garden in our yards, paint our homes, and turn down our rooms are often decidedly more memorable.

You and your team have the ability to increase your MQ by taking the seemingly unremarkable and making it Memorable.

The Legend of 9D

One of the perks of having dedicated 1.5 million miles to United Airlines is the ability to upgrade more times than not — a reward that I don't take lightly in this era of packed flights, reduced services, and full-body screening.

Joining me in business class or first, depending on the aircraft, is the typical assortment of business professionals and the occasional leisure traveler. The travelers find their seats, dive into their reading material, and frequently pay no attention to the other flyers that surround them.

Truth be told, that describes me. I covet the upgrade and keep to myself, rarely making small talk and not extending myself beyond the common human courtesy that should be an inherent part of air travel. After all, it's a dog-eat-dog world in the "friendly skies."

One day, as I settled in to prepare for the coast-to-coast journey ahead, the ground crew was assisting a passenger into his seat at the other end of my business class row.

He was a mess. Visibly black and blue, wearing a neck brace and a nose splint, and still displaying a hospital wristband, it was apparent that his last few days had not been some of his best.

The patient gingerly took his seat, reclined his chair, closed his eyes, and prepared for the long cross-country flight —

his journey made only slightly more comfortable, I assumed, by the fact that he did not have to sit in economy.

It was easy to guess that he was alone. However, a few moments later a woman appeared and said to the patient, "There is a seat next to me, although it does not recline as much, if you want to move." It seemed that his wife was seated in coach and, in an effort to care for him during the flight, was suggesting that he move to sit by her.

And that's when it happened.

The complete stranger sitting next to the patient in seat 9D looked at the woman and said, "Here, take my seat."

Somewhat stunned she replied, "I'm in economy."

He calmly offered, as he rose up from his *fully-reclining-42-inches-of-pitch-where-they-were-going-to-serve-edible-food-and-he-wouldn't-have-to-pay-for-cocktails* 9D seat. "That's OK, you should sit here."

And with that he made his way back to the dark recesses of economy — to sit in 17C.

The woman was dumbfounded, infinitely appreciative, and moved to tears.

The former occupant of 9D expected nothing in return; he simply recognized that someone was in need and rose up (literally) to help.

The woman's reward was an indelibly memorable moment wherein a complete stranger made a very difficult journey just a bit better.

The passenger in 9D had a reward that was arguably greater still — the quiet feeling of having made someone else's day that much better.

For his grand gesture, 9D, rather than being banished to economy, was expeditiously escorted by the flight attendant who witnessed his act of kindness to the cushy, comfortable private digs that only the fully flat reclining private pods and rarified air of United First could afford.

As it should be.

You're Invited: Wholesaler Pool Party

I've spoken *a lot* about PVP — Peerless Value Proposition®.

My coaching calls, speaking engagements, tele-classes, and radio shows have all addressed this topic.

And there is something important you need to know.

If you can't swim, stay out of the PVP water.

You see, in order to put your PVP into action, <u>you need to do more than what most wholesalers do.</u>

They put their toes into the PVP advisor waters simply by sitting on the edge of the pool, dangling their feet in the water — while holding a cocktail.

For them, it's a just a pool party.

Said another way, <u>they make a half-baked attempt</u> of developing and marketing the one thing <u>that will solidify</u> their MQ — Memorability Quotient® with their clients and prospects.

Coca-Cola does not take their brand development or the marketing of its brand lightly.

Neither do Apple, Porsche, Callaway, Budweiser, or *The Wall Street Journal.*

So why do you?

In some cases, wholesalers are just afraid to swim in the pool.

They believe they might get in over their heads and look foolish to their advisors.

They believe they don't have the creative skills to develop a solid PVP.

They believe they are too late to the PVP party because "everyone else is already doing it." (We heard that one yesterday.)

Let's be 100% clear.

The market is *crying out.*

Screaming, in fact!

Begging for you to be discernibly different than the last suit, with the last briefcase, who walked into the last office holding the same brochure with a different logo on it.

So we invite you to come to the wholesaler pool party — but we implore you to get into the PVP pool and swim out to the deep end.

What will you do to deftly create and market your PVP — Peerless Value Proposition®?

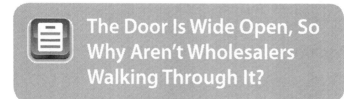
The Door Is Wide Open, So Why Aren't Wholesalers Walking Through It?

You know the game in sales.

You look for a crack in the door, wedge your foot in, and then work your butt off to blow the door wide open.

But what happens when the door is left open — *wide open*?!

I recall a 401(k) Rekon Advisor Symposium I hosted with 45 financial advisors in attendance.

They were a diverse group, mostly independent, with a smattering of wirehouse folks.

In addition to doing the Master of Ceremonies gig, I presented the "Five Ways Advisors Can Use Wholesalers to Get to Their Own Retirement."

They are:

1. Form Meaningful Partnerships
2. Understand the Wholesaler's PVP — Peerless Value Proposition®
3. Cooperatively Business Plan
4. Conduct Quarterly Checkpoint Sessions
5. Ask for What You Want

As I checked in with the advisors and polled them about wholesaler's behavior, it became all too clear that the door is wide open for the wholesaler who dares to be great.

For instance, I asked the audience how many of them had participated, at the wholesaler's request, in proactive business planning discussions.

Out of a room of 45 advisors, 3 raised their hands.

When polled about wholesalers doing checkpoint meetings to stay in touch with the "health" of their relationship with the advisor, I got blank stares — and not one hand went up even halfway.

More than ever, I am convinced that your ability to go from good wholesaler to great wholesaler isn't about herculean efforts.

It's simply about doing the stuff that other folks can't do.

Or won't do.

Or have become too complacent to do.

The door is wide open — when are you going to walk through it?

Just One Great Sales Idea

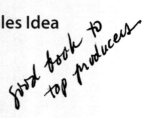
good book to top producers

You know Ben, right?

Benjamin Franklin, that is.

In 1758 he published a book called *The Way to Wealth*, written as a preface to *Poor Richard's Almanac*.

In only 30 pages, he delivers all of the goodness you'd expect from a guy who gets his picture on the hundred dollar bill.

In fact, this book is where two of Ben's all-time greatest hits come from:

> "Early to bed and early to rise makes a man healthy, wealthy, and wise."

> "There are no gains without pains."

And, if you read the book carefully, you'll find dozens more.

Idea: What if you bought copies for your Top 25 producers, inscribed the inside cover with a personal message and shot it out to them in the mail?

Think your MQ — Memorability Quotient® will go up?

Did Ben fly a kite?

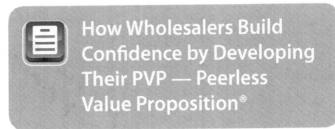

How Wholesalers Build Confidence by Developing Their PVP — Peerless Value Proposition®

Maybe you are a seasoned veteran who has lost a bit of your moxie.

Maybe you are a young wholesaler just starting out, somewhat tentatively, on the career journey.

In either case, developing a strong PVP — Peerless Value Proposition® can be just the medicine that you require to harness the confidence that you need.

Let me explain with one case study.

Jill (not her real name) is a wholesaler and coaching client who has been in the field for less than one year, and she confides that she's not adding any value to the advisors she calls on.

Note: I don't care what your feeling is about the word "value" (as so many folks apologize for using it), but the reality is if Jill feels she's not adding it, she's got a problem to address.

When introduced to the concept of PVP, Jill first suggests that she'd be hard pressed to find what hers would be.

So I peppered her with questions that revealed a true passion that Jill has for helping advisors construct effective, risk-adjusted, and favorably performing portfolios.

In fact, I learned that Jill lives and breathes the topic.

She reads and listens to more about the topic than most.

The acid test question came when I asked her if she could hold her own with *any* advisor, young or old, when it came to the topic and she exclaimed, "Yes!" almost immediately.

In fact, this was the point where Jill got a huge uptick in her confidence.

She realized that while she might be newer on the whole-saling scene, she had a talent that would allow her to stand toe to toe with advisors *and* become a truly valuable resource to their business.

And that is just one brilliant by-product of discovering and harnessing your PVP.

So tell me, what's your PVP — Peerless Value Proposition®?

7 Ways Wholesalers Can Market Like Coca-Cola

What if you had the ability to become the Coca-Cola of your region?

A force so large that other brands (wholesalers) get cold sweats just thinking about squaring off against you.

A brand (you) so prevalent that virtually most advisors were drawn to your offering.

Just how powerful is the Coca-Cola brand?

Consider this (source: businessinsider.com):

- Of the 55 billion servings of all kinds of beverages drunk each day (other than water), 1.7 billion are Coca-Cola trademarked/licensed drinks — and that's 3.1%.

- Coca-Cola has reported that its name is the second-most understood term in the world, behind "okay."

- There are 33 non-alcoholic brands that each generate over $1 billion in revenue. Coca-Cola owns a whopping 15 of them.

In order to get to that level of stature, of course you need great product.

And you also need a great PVP — Peerless Value Proposition®.

Something that no one else in the market can do — and if they do it, they don't do it as well as you.

In their 2011 Annual Review Coke states, "Our business was built for times like these. We provide consumers with an affordable luxury: we sell moments of happiness."

And no one is marketing those moments of happiness better than Coke.

In fact, they will have spent approximately $11 billion on marketing in 2012.

So how can you, with a well formulated PVP — Peerless Value Proposition®, market like Coca-Cola — minus the $10,999,950,000?

To attack your marketing like Coke, first consider all the different mediums available to spread your message — which if you're Coke includes:

- TV
- Radio
- Sports Team Sponsorship
- Magazine
- Product Placement
- Web
- Social Media

Translated to your wholesaling practice, you have the opportunity every day to market your PVP through:

1. **Sales meetings:** Every time you stand in front of a group of advisors you are given the chance to reinforce your PVP.

   Put a powerful PVP descriptor into your introduction.

2. **Centers of Influence:** Use your PVP to develop a deeper level of interest in you/your firm with your COIs.

   We know that they care about product — they just don't care that much.

   What they do care about more is how, through your PVP, you will help their team sell more stuff and make more money.

3. **One on one:** Every visit, with every advisor, gives you a chance to speak about an element of your PVP and how it can accrete to their goals and objectives.

4. **Email marketing:** A well constructed PVP, and accompanying marketing plan, gives you content that translates into emails that get opened and read.

   Instead of emails that have a singular product focus, your <u>emails now have a value focus</u>.

5. **Outgoing voice mail:** Trying to get an appointment with a new advisor?

   Leaving the same old ineffective "I'll be in your neighborhood and want to stop by" message?

   Stop!

Try infusing your message with your PVP and use that as the cornerstone for why the advisor should take time to meet with you.

6. **Incoming voice mail:** Use your recorded voice mail message on your cell phone to promote your brand.

   (Check out "8 Ways Wholesalers Can Best Use Voice Mail as a Sales Tool" later in this section.)

7. **Internal Wholesaler coordinated "ads":** Make absolutely certain that your internal shares your vision for your PVP and is able to articulate its benefits for the advisors they touch every day.

But it all begins with your PVP — Peerless Value Proposition®.

You need to have one that is solid, will open doors, and can be the platform for the marketing efforts you wish to undertake.

 The Lowest Paying White-Collar Job

The noble bank teller.

In the late 1970s, that's how I started my journey in financial services.

Banks were just starting to interject "sales" into the retail bank formula.

So, we were taught to cross-sell — and offered statistics about how the stickiness of a client relationship was directly correlated to the number of services the client had.

Checking only	=	high risk to leave
Checking + mortgage loan + auto loan + CD	=	high likelihood to stay

And so it is with wholesaling.

Product spewing guy/gal	=	advisor has high likelihood to leave you when your product falls out of favor

Meaningful to the advisor relationship on multiple levels:

Practice management, your PVP – Peerless Value Proposition®, case/ portfolio design, staff training, etc.	=	advisor has high likelihood to weather performance or pricing speed bumps

The Typical Wholesaler vs the Great Wholesaler — An Infographic

The simple fact is that I get to coach truly outstanding folks.

In a discussion with one of those clients, we were lamenting how difficult it is for wholesalers to separate themselves from the Sea of Sameness and measurably increase their MQ — Memorability Quotient®.

Part of the challenge lies in simple DNA.

If you are an analytical person by nature then you are going to naturally default to the numbers and theory of our business.

If you are a creative personality then getting into the product weeds will be much more difficult for you.

The biggest challenge is that <u>becoming more well-rounded takes a *ton* of work</u> — work that the typical wholesaler is unwilling to do.

As a result, the conversational ability that they have with advisors looks like this:

Conversely, Great Wholesalers painstakingly apply themselves to their unique ability to lead an advisor down any number of conversational paths — and they do so seamlessly and elegantly.

As a result, the conversational ability that they have with advisors looks like this:

GREAT WHOLESALERS

I have a reasonably good idea about where you aspire to be.

Now look in the mirror and answer only to yourself — where are you today?

Wholesalers, what's your PVP — Peerless Value Proposition®?

Welcome to the Wholesaler Beauty Pageant

You've been invited to speak at a sales meeting.

According to the sales manager, there should be 30 advisors in attendance.

In exchange for your "support" (read: $200) you will have a solid 15 minutes to pitch whatever you want.

Oh, and the manager tells you that you will be one of six wholesalers on the agenda.

Welcome to the *Wholesaler Beauty Pageant*.

No pressure, but how do you intend to stand out in this *sea of wholesaling sameness*?

It's guaranteed that one or more of the other five wholesalers will:

- Open with a line similar to, "Thanks for having me to the meeting." Or worse, "I'm the only thing between you and _____ (drinks, golf, dinner, going home)." Not having prepared or practiced what they are about to spew forth.

- Offer a long, tired, old sales idea.

- Pitch a random product that has the highest Morningstar ranking while stressing performance against the index, benchmark, competitors, etc.

- Look like they shopped for their business wardrobe at Target and had not had their shoes shined in, well, ever.

So what will you do?

You could: ✔

- Deliver insightful comments about the state of the economy, your firm's outlook, and how advisors should be positioned with their clients.

- Offer a solid business building/practice management idea that you have gleaned from your extensive travels and discussions with advisors "just like them."

- Formulate a talk that has greater intensity, humor, insight, compelling stories, or captivating visuals that will actually stick with the advisor two minutes after you're off the stage.

- Make a bold statement.

- Challenge a traditional assumption.

- Create some controversy.

We both know that the "cavalcade of wholesalers" meeting is one of the hardest to break through.

You'll shine through if you have a plan, preparation, practice, and performance.

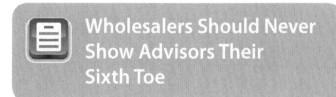
"Your best client is also your competitor's best prospect!"

That was the familiar refrain we used to hear from our sales manager.

And, of course, she was right.

So what can you do to make sure that your top producers remain *your* top producers?

While a host of ideas are explored throughout this book, the #1 suggestion is:

> Never get too close, and don't get too comfortable with advisors!

Our jobs are to form relationships.

So, does it run counter to the job to not get too close to an advisor?

In a word, no.

Think about it this way. You are single (married folks, pretend) and you meet a great guy/girl who seems to be the complete package. Looks, brains, sense of humor are all 8+ on the 1-10 scale.

So you start the courtship.

Somewhere along the line, after you get *a lot* more comfortable, you have an occasion to be bare footed (let your mind wander) and great guy/gal notices that you have six toes.

Since you are not that rich or that funny (see Drew Carey and his sixth toe), great guy/gal is repulsed and the courtship ends — and you are not even left with a friendship.

Similarly, why get so close to an advisor that they can see your sixth toe? Even though we all have them (metaphorically speaking) they can be kept in the comfort of a sock and no one is the wiser.

What's too comfortable/too close behavior with a rep you ask?

Here are three that should ring true for all wholesalers:

- Drinking to excess which, in turn, makes you do dumb things, or worse
- Debating political views
- Over-sharing religious beliefs

true!

So go out and form the tightest relationships possible with as many advisors as you can — but let the other wholesaler show their sixth toe.

At the beginning of every quarter, I ask my coaching clients what successes they were most proud of from the prior quarter's work.

A Wholesaler Masterminds private coaching client (we'll call him Clark) told me a terrific story and I need to tell you.

Back in March 2010, Clark set up a meeting to visit a Raymond James team with approximately $200 million under management. As he was newer to wholesaling he went into the meeting admittedly less prepared than he might have liked, but willing to put it on the line to rope in this team's business — they were Elephants.

Clark attempted to go into his pitch and was cut off by the team — stopped dead in his tracks.

They said, "You are going about this all wrong."

The team then made an offer to Clark.

They said that they model their practice on their Nick Murray learnings and told Clark that if he was willing to read two books of Nick's in the upcoming 90 days that they would be willing to set up another meeting with him; believing that having read the books Clark would better understand how they operate.

So what did Clark do?

He read the two books; then he scheduled a follow-up meeting.

In that meeting, he spent 45 minutes learning about the team's practice, how they manage money, how they interact with their clients, along with a host of other insights.

When Clark was done, the team said, "Welcome. You are now a part of *our* team."

Clark asked for their product matrix to analyze where his funds might fit — and they gave it to him.

He set up a call for the next week with the Raymond James team and his fund family's portfolio managers to discuss a potential $10 to $30 million allocation.

I asked Clark why he thought that this team gave him this remarkable second chance. He offered a few suggestions as to why.

1. At no point was he an arrogant wholesaler.
2. When the team pushed back, he did not get defensive.
3. He took the time to listen.
4. He followed through on their suggestion to read the books.
5. The team appreciated him for being younger and willing to learn — and they wanted to help.

The wholesaling landscape is littered with guys and gals who are getting their teeth kicked in every day.

It's so great to hear success stories like this that validate the very reason why we do what we do.

Wholesaler Masterminds clients are a breed apart.

The Four Cs of the Legendary Wholesaler

My wholesaling experience goes back to the dark ages.

Yes, it was BC — Before Cell.

From time to time I speak to a wholesaler who now works in some part of my old region(s) and they tell me they have reps who remember me and the work that I did.

That means two things.

One, those advisors are old like me.

Two, I must have left an impression on them.

In fact, I was blown away to receive this random comment on a blog post recently. It came from an advisor that I have not seen nor talked to in more than 15 years.

> Mr. Shore: Been a very long time. See that you are still doing what you do best, educating the sales force. Just wanted to say hello to you. Thought about you a lot over the years. You made an everlasting impression on me and I'm sure it's the same with your coaching and training today. Glad to see things are good with you.

One of the wholesalers I spoke to used the word "legendary," but let's be perfectly clear: Legendary is a massively large word and my head is *not* that big!

But it did get me thinking.

What will your advisors say about you after you've moved on?

What will you do to be thought of as legendary?

Big question, I know.

At Wholesaler Masterminds we think part of the answer is found in the Four Cs.

1. **Connect:** Legendary wholesalers have the ability to connect with a broad array of advisors.

   This is where that chameleon-like quality comes into play.

   It doesn't matter to the legendary wholesaler that the advisor is male or female, Democrat or Republican, game hunter or vegan — they have the unique ability to not just "get along with the advisor" but to speak their language and engage in dialog that appeals to the advisor's interests.

2. **Convey:** Educating advisors about macro-economic and world events keeps a legendary wholesaler on top of things.

   Help them understand the granular details of the fund, policy, or contract offered by your firm.

   Give them valuable how to's that save them time and trouble when they sell your product.

   All qualities of the legendary wholesaler.

3. **Compel:** Legendary wholesalers move people to action.

   They offer advisors "best of" product presentations that are client-focused and weave a great tale, versus the repetitive feature-benefit-feature-benefit blather that also-ran wholesalers spew.

   Their unique ability to simplify the most complex concepts into easy-to-understand ideas make them an in-demand speaker at group meetings, client seminars, and industry events.

   They command a room with their story-telling prowess.

4. **Close:** Even legendary wholesalers are in sales.

   And your advisors are in sales.

   The legendary wholesaler understands this and doesn't hesitate to close for the business that they have earned the right to ask for.

   They also understand that there is a line between pleasantly persistent and pushy; consultative and cocky.

   But make no mistake they know how to close.

So, was I a legendary wholesaler?

I'll let the advisors that I served be the judge of that.

How will you be judged?

As I sat in the audience of the 2010 Sequoia Connect conference and listened to each Wholesaler Lifetime Achievement Award winner speak from the dais, I couldn't help but make a list of the attributes that they outlined as being most critical to their success.

The words/phrases in **bold** are the award winner's descriptions of what attributes make wholesalers great. The explanations that follow each are our take on each attribute.

- **Competitive:** Each wholesaler has a different button that they need pushed. What's yours?

  Do you seek to make more money than any of your peers?

  Or are you driven by the acclaim that the highest achievers receive?

  Wholesalers should not only know what gets them revved up (the easy part), they should also find a way to let their boss in on the secret.

  One time I had a wholesaler who I thought was motivated by money as her number one driver.

  Wrong!

  It turned out that recognition was her number one most important measuring/motivating device.

Whatever your "button," the very best are tenaciously competitive in their pursuit.

🔹 **Able to build teams:** Sure, wholesaling is a lone wolf engagement, designed for the guy/gal who really wants to do their thing and not have to be concerned with that whole "team" thing ... right?

To put this gently — *Hell No!*

In this era of wholesaling, you need to ditch that idea and get with the *team* program.

This means that you have the ability to orchestrate and/or add input into the activities of all those who touch your region.

That includes your internal (of course), any sales assistant(s), relationship management, and other wholesalers from complimentary products in your firm (retirement plans, life, etc.) to name a few.

🔹 **Loves to meet people:** You might be thinking, "Really, there are wholesalers who don't like to meet people?"

Maybe, but the key here is the word *love*.

There are plenty of folks who claim to be "a people person," but under the hood they are simply putting up with the social demands of the job.

Those who are great wholesalers love the social aspect of the job — and it shows.

🔹 **Strongest possible work ethic:** Though it's been said before, we'll say it again: Wholesaling is not just a job; it is a lifestyle.

And a lifestyle that demands a work ethic that borders on sickness if you plan to reach the top.

No, it does not mean forsaking family and friends to reach the top, as there are important ways to work smarter.

Yes, it does require a degree of commitment that only a rare percentage are willing to relent to.

And in this millennium you better be working hard because there are three or more folks waiting to take your job from you.

- **Constantly seeking feedback from advisors on ways to improve:** We'll take this one step further and say that great wholesalers are not only seeking feedback from advisors on ways to improve, but they are also seeking this input from their peers and from their boss.

  The very best also seek the counsel of outside coaches — *yup, shameless plug!*

  Regardless of who they hear it from, great wholesalers listen, process, and improve.

  They *listen* with an open mind.

  They *process* what they have heard before they act/react.

  They use their new learnings, take them to heart, and they *improve*.

- **The greatest wholesalers are highly motivated:** They are the folks who get out of bed in the morning and can't wait to get busy. More times than not, the motivation for these wholesalers is radiating from the inside out — they have a burning desire and it fuels their everyday activities.

This means that their thoughts remain mostly positive and their actions continue to propel them mostly forward.

Through this motivation, they gather up the persistence, inspiration, tenacity, and energy required to achieve at a high level — day after day.

- **The best of the best view wholesaling as a game:** While sports analogies are not for everyone and can be grossly overdone, the parallels are compelling.

  Games require a strategy and a plan.

  They teach us patience.

  We learn to work in cooperation with others.

  And, if your game of choice is football, ice hockey, boxing, etc., "games" also provide us with instruction about how to get up off the ground, dust ourselves off, and keep fighting.

- **Enjoy relationships:** Can you be a successful wholesaler and not? It's debatable.

  The very best in our field covet, cultivate, and nurture the relationships that they know will be accretive to their success.

  And they work their hardest to form strong bonds with their best advisors and COIs (Centers of

Influence) such that the strength of the relationship forms a barrier to competitive entry.

 Extremely coachable: Your managers want to work with wholesalers who will respond to training and mentoring.

The superstar wholesaler knows that the only way to improve, to expand, and to flourish over a long period of time is to be open and available for feedback.

Gone are the days of the rogue wholesaler "who does things her way" and ignores the role that solid feedback/coaching/mentoring can play.

These wholesalers know that coaching comes in many forms.

Whether receiving feedback from their immediate boss, a trusted colleague, or a paid consultant, great wholesalers know that they need to "get out of their own head" and get constructive input — regardless of their present level of success.

Often you'll hear great wholesalers talk about the *thrill of the sale*. They love to "hunt" for the ticket, contract, policy, or plan.

Does a deal give you a buzz?

Does a bigger deal give you a bigger buzz?

That's the thrill — and it's what the very best chase.

All day.

Every day.

They Made the Cable Company Look Good

Maybe I should still be a renter.

Reason being, when stuff breaks you call the landlord.

The repair de jour is now the U-Line wine fridge and the Thermadore oven — in order of priority!

The repair service I called gave me a 3-hour window (bad sign) and at the 2-hour and 55-minute mark I called to ask where they were.

"We'll be there within 30 minutes," was the reply.

To which I said, "If I wanted to be made to feel like my business didn't matter I would have scheduled the cable company!!"

Next time you know you are running late for an appointment for heaven's sake proactively call — don't just show up late, even if it's only five minutes.

Sound basic?

Yes.

Does everyone do it?

Absolutely not.

Simple, not easy, way to increase your MQ – Memorability Quotient®?

No doubt.

3 Things Wholesalers Do to Impress Home Office Visitors

Recently, a coaching client informed me that he had his boss coming for a ride-along.

My first question was, "How many appointments do you have?"

His answer was not pretty.

What about you?

You get the call that your boss, or any home office person, will be coming into your region — now what?

This could be someone from:

- Product Management
- Marketing
- Portfolio Management
- Underwriting
- Executive Management (CEO, President, etc.)

Unfortunately, some wholesalers do not understand the weight of this visit.

Whether they realize it or not, their reputation will either be enhanced by this visit or diminished — because the fact is that this visitor will talk about you when they get back to the home office.

There are three primary takeaways that you need to be sure they marvel at:

1. **How hard you work:** Your goal is simple.

    You want the visitor astounded by the sheer volume of your work.

    Pick them up early.

    Drop them off late.

    Crush them in between.

    But it's not just the quantity that counts — it's also the quality.

2. **The breadth of your knowledge:** You should be known as the walking/talking encyclopedia of information about your product and your firm already.

    With a visitor present, it's time to let that light of knowledge shine as brightly as possible.

    Seek out meetings where you can dazzle folks with your brilliance.

3. **The depth of your relationships:** From the rookies to the "corner office."

    From the receptionist to the Big(gest) Kahuna — everyone is familiar with you, your product, your firm, and your value.

    Introduce your guest to everyone in the food chain.

    When your guest leaves, they'll believe you could make a bona fide run for mayor!

Make it your primary goal to have that visitor shaking their head in awe of what you do — and telling everyone in the home office about it.

How will you impress the heck out of your next visitor from the home office?

 CEO, Oh No!

"Rob, the CEO is coming to SoCal and wants to ride with you."

Panic.

Followed by anxiety.

With a side helping of fear.

That's a proper recounting of the emotions as I remember them when the then CEO of OppenheimerFunds came to visit.

As he was a high profile industry leader, my internal and I left no stone unturned — making sure the anchor meeting of his visit, an open invitation breakfast meeting at an LAX hotel, was promoted to death.

If you were a producer, prospect, or COI we made sure you knew about the visit ... multiple times.

The venue was selected — not too expensive mind you, as this CEO was thrifty.

The catering contract with the hotel was signed.

The marketing materials were delivered.

On the day of the event, the room was carefully set for the 60 RSVPs.

Showtime!

And a grand total of 12 advisors showed up.

TWELVE!

Mortified, I spent the balance of his visit apologizing, certain my budding career was about to wilt.

Fortunately for me, he took it in stride.

5 Things to Do to Make COIs Love You

Centers of Influence (COI) come in all shapes and sizes.

Regardless of your channel or your product, great wholesalers know that these folks can make the difference between good years and great years.

Here's a list of things to do to make COIs love you.

1. **Ask for and understand their goals:** Way too many wholesalers are "me" focused when they should be "COI-centric." When was the last time you sat down with a branch manager, complex manager, IMO, district manager, etc., and asked them about *their* goals?

   - How much gross are they expected to produce?
   - What is their recruitment target?
   - Is there a particular product mix they are trying to achieve?

   Don't expect the keys to the COI kingdom if all you do is focus on you.

2. **Find out where they have pain:** Are you aware of the challenges that your COI faces?

   As an example, every manager has x% of producers who are on the fence about hitting their goals. And they have assorted pressures that they are managing from their boss and the home office. If you find out what those issues are and help to find solutions you, my friend, are not just another wholesaler.

You are now a business consultant.

3. **Commit to communication:** How valuable would it be to a COI if you were able to keep them in the loop regarding

- the number of appointments you had in their shop?
- the kinds of questions that you are getting most frequently from advisors?
- the products that seem to be getting the most interest from producers?
- the issues that are preventing business — any kind of business — from being written?
- the "first responder" communications that explain important events (think "Flash Crash")?

Put your COIs on speed dial, both metaphorically and literally.

Send them email updates.

Communicate.

4. **Cooperative planning:** This is the perfect time to get with your most prized COIs and formulate a game plan for the year ahead.

They want practice management ideas, advanced product training, and conversion to fee-based business assistance.

You have solutions — both from within your firm and from your vast resources.

5. **Follow through relentlessly:** You know our mantra: *Do what you say you're going to do, when you say you're going do it.*

   The chart that follows gives you some idea of how wide open this opportunity is for the great wholesaler.

Are your COIs in love with you?

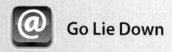

Go Lie Down

Have you ever built a house or done a major remodel?

If yes, then you know the builder "walk through."

If not, stay with me anyway.

In a newly built home, this is where you are handed a tick-sheet and asked to go through the house and note any of the issues that the builder needs to resolve.

One of my co-workers suggested laying face up on the floor in the middle of each room.

He said that when you lay on the floor you'll observe things from that perspective that you would other-wise miss from a conventional viewpoint.

Go ahead. Try it.

Never noticed that nail pop in the drywall did you?

Taking on this different angle sharpens your powers of observation.

How keen are your wholesaling powers of observation?

One time I was calling on the head of product for a gigantic broker/dealer that our firm needed to secure. The meeting took place in the product manager's office and I had one of my wholesalers with me.

When we left the meeting he started rattling off all of the things that he had observed in her office.

The folks in her pictures.

The books on her shelves.

The knick-knacks on her credenza.

We then discussed ways to forge a relationship with her based on what we had seen.

Do you need to sharpen your powers of observation?

23 Client Event Ideas for Wholesalers to Use with Advisors

Pulling off a successful client event is no easy task.

And we've been getting a lot of inquiries lately about suggestions for great client events.

In this post, we define "client" as the public customer and/or the advisor.

As an example, we have wholesaler coaching clients using some of these ideas to enhance the normally mundane and poorly attended wirehouse lunch meeting.

These ideas have varying degrees of relevance depending on your channel, geography, demographics, time of year, etc.

That said, the plain truth is that your ability to implement a terrific event successfully can have long-term benefits that go on for years.

1. **Wine Tasting:** Have you listened to the Wholesaler Masterminds Radio show "Conducting Wildly Successful Wholesaler Sponsored Wine Events?"

2. **Cooking Classes:** Either onsite with a private chef or offsite at a cooking school location, such as Sur La Table.

3. **Pumpkin Patch:** Bring the farm to the advisor's office.

4. **Pumpkin Carving:** … and teach folks how to make their own Jack-O-Lanterns.

5. **Gift Wrapping Classes:** Contact a local department store's manager and ask if they can send a gift wrapper.

6. **Botany Lessons:** There isn't a plant in my house that has ever lasted more than a week. A professional botanist can address that as well as outdoor gardens. Call a Home Depot, Armstrong's or your local gardening center. Also, your local college may have experts to call upon.

7. **Quilting (or Knitting) Lessons:** Not my thing, and maybe not yours, but quilting is huge.

8. **Paper Shredding:** This one event ranks as a tremendous way for advisors to get clients to come out — even those who often don't show for anything else. Hire a professional shredding service that brings one of their trucks to your advisor's locations and let the confetti fly.

9. **Identity Theft Clinic:** Check with your local police department or FBI office and have an expert come out and give a 45-minute session on how to avoid identity theft.

10. **Golf Lessons:** Rather than doing it at a range, arrange for a pro to come to the office and do a clinic. Sand

traps, short game, putting — rent a virtual simulator to jazz up the event further.

11. **Poker Lessons:** There are a ton of amateur poker enthusiasts everywhere. What about having a local poker pro come out and give lessons/tips?

12. **Fashion Update:** Skinny ties and no pleated slacks? Or is it rounded shoes versus pointy ones? Have a local personal shopper come out, from Nordstrom for example, and educate the audience on what's in and what's out.

13. **Jewelry or Watch Show:** Contact a local high-end watch shop or jeweler and have a swanky event for clients. Serve a bit of bubbly and higher end canapés.

14. **Car Show:** Call your local Mercedes or BMW dealer and tell them that you'd like a fleet manager to come out with a couple of the latest and greatest models. Believe me, they're not going to say no.

15. **Great Food Truck Event:** Have you seen the show on Food Network called the *Great Food Truck Race*? In many cities, food trucks are all the rage, and the food is great! Why not sponsor a food truck event?

16. **iPad/iPhone Tips and Tricks:** There's a reason Apple had blow out earnings numbers — their products are amazing. Why not contact a local Apple Store and see if a Genius is available to come out and do a tips-and-tricks clinic.

17. **Social Media Clinic:** My Dad is 83 and on Facebook. Your clients are trying to decipher how to use social media for either their personal or business use. Find a local "expert" (because there are about a million self-proclaimed social media experts) who can address your questions.

18. **E-Waste Collection:** The local YMCA had one of these lately and it was busy. Clients are invited to bring all their old TVs, computers, monitors, etc., and know that they will be properly disposed of by a professional recycling company.

19. **Final Days Symposium:** Kind of morbid I know, but we are all going to die. This session would bring in mortuary spokespeople, estate attorneys, and long-term care specialists.

20. **Life Coach/Life Balance:** Most folks are running as fast as they can to have the career they want, the family they want, and the down time they have earned. Naturally, some level of stress ensues. Hire a life coach to address living in balance.

21. **Career Transition Clinic:** More and more, folks are redefining their idea of retirement — and for most sitting on white sand beaches for 24/7/365 is not a part of it. Many wish to continue to work but want to shift the "how." Corporate expats move to entrepreneurship, full-time women move to part time to accommodate a family, seniors working part time. And they all need advice along the way.

22. **Social Security Administration Update:** For as long as we have been affiliated with wholesaling, this has been a topic that draws a crowd. The good news is that the SSA has this form to fill out to request a speaker. The bad news is that it's a form on a government website. Who knows where it goes?

23. **Medicare Update:** See #22 as it's the same concept, the same draw for clients and the same form — you simply change the drop down for the subject you are looking for.

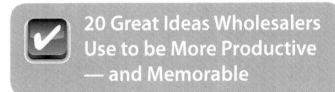

20 Great Ideas Wholesalers Use to be More Productive — and Memorable

This list was distilled from coaching calls, feedback from readers, and input from advisors over too many hours to count.

The ideas presented here only scratch the surface of the depth and breadth of knowledge, experience, and wisdom great wholesalers apply in their practice every day.

1. Most wholesalers have no agenda when they arrive at a rep's office. Great wholesalers send an email prior to advisor appointments asking what the advisor wants to discuss, issues they have, and questions on their mind. Check out the Delay Send Feature in MS Outlook.

2. We see LinkedIn as the de facto place to build our community, and yet we still see wholesalers who either are not present on the site or have weak presence. Check out articles (and audios) at Wholesaler Masterminds to get great information about how to craft an effective profile. In addition, make certain that you are a member of the Wholesaler Masterminds Group at LinkedIn.

3. Handwritten Thank You cards get noticed now more than ever. We have clients using SendOutCards.

While their business model is multilevel marketing, they do have Pay As You Go plans.

4. Handwritten Thank You cards that are specific to an advisor's interest (wine, golf, NASCAR, etc.) are a home run every time.

5. Dictate your call notes, thank you cards, follow-up letters from your phone right after your appointment. We've used Copytalk and the Dragon Dictation iPhone app with great success. And we've used Copytalk to dictate newsletters and blog posts. The accuracy of the dictation and the speed of turnaround are both good.

6. Good wholesalers ask for referrals. Great wholesalers ask for referrals *and* deliver feedback to the referrer *on* the progress of those referrals.

7. Develop a "Fallen Angels" list. Stratify that list by asset class, product, firm, producer level, and by geography. Another list to have is your Ten Most Wanted list and one tactic to re-engage producers is with lists of their clients invested in your products that you hand deliver.

8. Business planning with advisors is a waste of time without firm business commitments. Tell them how much you need from them in dollars. Also use the the Top X method of requesting a commitment. "Bill, I'd love to say that you are a top 10 producer in my region and that requires you to commit to $5 million in business. Are you in?" See also "Great Wholesalers: 8 Ways to Always Be Closing" in Part Three.

9. Old school marketing used fax blasts. New school marketing uses VoiceShot. Also try Call-Em-Call.

10. Joint client appointments allow you to display your brilliance. Great wholesalers press for them. Great wholesalers also host terrific and memorable client events too (see "23 Client Event Ideas for Wholesalers to Use with Advisors" earlier in this section).

11. A good, albeit common, question to ask: "What cases are you working on?" A great, consultative question to ask: "What cases have you missed on?"

12. Keep your internal, your scheduler, and your admin (you have one right?) all on the same page with Google Drive. Share calendars, spread sheets, etc.

13. Loops, zones, sub-zones are great. And sometimes a great wholesaler has to set a follow-up appointment for hot prospects sooner than the rotation would otherwise dictate.

14. Run advisors' preferred fund grid through an analytic screen like FI360 to see where your product better fills their style needs.

15. For a phone call that requires a visual (PowerPoint, charts, graphs, tours of brochures, etc.) use Glance. It's a simple, low-cost way to bring your spoken word to life. Also a super simple and free way to share your screen has arrived. Check out join.me.

16. For your VIP advisors host an exclusive client call with a portfolio manager.

17. To find outsource help (virtual assistants, admin support, etc.), explore elance.com or HireMyMom.com, which is where I found my assistant.

18. Take the time to comb through the valuable data that your firm provides and know your territory, and its weak spots, thoroughly. Use IXI or use Market Metric's new product which might be a category killer as it allows you to dial into production in your region in a way that has not been possible in the past.

19. Focus on relationship building with Centers of Influence. See "8 Ways Wholesalers Succeed with COIs" in Part One and "5 Things to Do to Make COIs Love You" earlier in this section.

20. Stay in front of the information tsunami with RSS. Learn how to use Google Reader. We've added a live news feed at Wholesaler Masterminds. Choose between Think Like An Advisor, Financial News Stream, Blogs You Should Be Reading, and Business Life. Use the app Feeddler to view your Google Reader feed on your smart phone or tablet.

And that's just a sample.

Are you being as productive (and memorable) as possible?

5 Ways Wholesalers Develop More Openable and Readable Emails

How many emails do you get in a day?

A week?

How backlogged are you in reading them?

In a recent meeting with a prospect, I asked if she had received an email I had sent.

She said, "Maybe." And added, "It might be in my 'read later' folder."

Which, while not an email death sentence, is the email equivalent of life behind bars.

So, what's a well intentioned wholesaler to do when trying to reach a financial advisor via email, especially knowing that email marketing is a fantastic way to increase your PVP — Peerless Value Proposition®?

How do you rise up out of the in-box Sea of Email Sameness?

Simple.

My Sunday Night Email series are consistently opened by over 40% of recipients, and we deliver to over 10,000 folks every week. So use the rules we employ.

1. **Create an irresistible subject line.**

   If you are on the Sunday Night Email list you are familiar with some of our titles:

   - Ones Is Better than Nones
   - Deciding Between 4½ and 4½
   - Laila Wanted Me Fired
   - Pool Man Jumped the Shark
   - Bad Decisions in Bozeman

   Another example, one of our best read stories was titled "Sushi, Sake, See Ya!" (read it in Part Four).

   It was a story about the need for managers to give *all* producers constructive and candid feedback — even their top performers.

   It could have easily been titled "Managers Should Offer Better Feedback" — and it would have been read less than 60% as much as it was — because the subject line got it opened.

   Want to invite the rep to a roadshow?

   Forgettable email subject line: "Join Us On May 7th"

   Email that gets opened: "What Do Foonman Funds and Cirque du Soleil Have in Common?"

   Want the advisor to look at a sales idea that's attached?

   Forgettable email subject line: "How Foonman Funds' Smid Cap Fund Performs in All Markets"

   Email that gets opened: "Smurfs, Smores and … Smids"

Next time you are crafting an email message, pay more attention to the subject line.

2. Grab them with your first sentence.

Make the first sentence "bite size."

Why?

Because we are all scanners.

We want to know if the words that follow will entice us to read more.

The Sunday Night Email series has openers such as:

- *I've admitted it before, I'll admit it again: I tend to be a workaholic.*

- *Too much food. Too much wine. Too much fun.*

- *Shortcomings. We all have them.*

3. Tell a story.

Everybody likes stories.

So why should advisors be forced to read the same, tired emails from you?

You know, the one that says:

Foonman Funds is proud to announce that the All Africa Small Cap Utilities Fund has just received its fifth star from Morningstar. Our portfolio manager, when asked about the regions utility outlook says …

Somebody shoot me now.

Instead, wrap up a message in a story:

Being a portfolio manager entails more than one risk.

"By 2 AM, our four seater, single-engine plane was about to run out of fuel as we landed hard and a bit too fast in Zomba Airport on our way to the largest Malawi electric plant."

That's how our All Africa Small Cap Utilities Fund manager started his recent investor call.

4. Use a P.S.

Our eyes naturally gravitate to the postscript in an email (or snail mail) first.

So why not use that section — and use it for a great offer, important message, or anything else that you want to make sure has a higher degree of likelihood to get read.

5. Find your voice.

You don't need to have studied creative writing in school.

But you should work on creating your own unique "voice" with your emails so that they further stand out from the Sea of In-box Sameness.

And, when done right, you may even have folks who actually look forward to your communications.

**How can you make more of an
impact with email?**

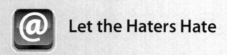 **Let the Haters Hate**

Marketing your wholesaling practice is tricky.

And the more you market, the more you'll have folks who don't get your style, message, or method.

Marketing through email is trickier.

And every once in a while I get flamed by a hater who finds the content of my Sunday Night Emails irrelevant, offensive, poorly timed, or they're just plain ticked off at the world.

Thankfully (and I am thankful), 99% of the feedback I get from readers about the weekly emails is incredibly positive.

But this I know — and I know it even more now after listening to a recent interview with advisors about what they want from wholesalers:

> Advisors prefer email as their primary form
> of communication with wholesalers.

But, as the advisors on the call mentioned, they want that digital content to be relevant.

And personalized.

And insightful.

And not filled with canned garbage like too many emails in our in-boxes are filled with.

So, let the haters hate.

You keep thoughtfully and creatively marketing to grow your practice.

8 Ways Wholesalers Can Best Use Voice Mail as a Sales Tool

Every day, I call wholesalers at a host of firms, in virtually all channels, and I continue to be astounded by how few take advantage of voice mail as any kind of selling tool.

In fact, sometimes I'm not even certain that I have reached their business line — a function of the wholesaler failing to mention the name of their firm.

Why not tackle one business building idea that is relatively painless and takes mere moments to implement.

1. **Set the right tone:** Boring, somber tones of voice don't make me look forward to the real you. Accurately represent who you are in your message. It can be as simple as making sure you smile while you record the message. Yes, it sounds odd — and yes, it *always* works.

2. **Reference your firm name and, optionally, your region:** I *know* it's basic — and folks frequently still don't do it.

3. **Give the caller a taste of something that represents your unique brand statement:** Our Wholesaler Masterminds clients know that we always emphasize having a uniqueness (their PVP — Peerless Value Proposition®) that defines them well beyond their

firm and product. Why not incorporate this into the message?

4. **Preview a product that is of interest:** Tease callers with a sound bite regarding a product feature that they might want to hear more about when you do speak live.

5. **Highlight a service that will get attention:** This could be an upcoming road show, seminar series, or portfolio manager call.

6. **Let folks know what to expect:** Outline when callers can expect to hear back from you. And for heaven's sake don't screw this up or your credibility will be shot.

7. **Tell them what you need to get from them:** Ask for their number (even if they know you have it) so you can keep to a minimum freeway collisions caused by looking up numbers. Why not also ask for the best time to call? Getting that information will help reduce exhausting games of phone tag.

8. **Give callers the opportunity to opt out or bypass your message:** Frankly I am iffy on this one. It flies in the face of some of the other suggestions — and yet if you have nothing valuable to offer in your message it's a nice feature for the caller to have.

Here's a sample message using the points outlined above (underlined):

You've reached <u>Rob Shore</u> with <u>Foonman Funds</u> in <u>LA/OC</u>. If you'll <u>leave me your number and best time</u>

to call, I'll get back to you by the end of the business day. When we do speak, remind me to tell you about the three critical client acquisition strategies that my most successful advisors are using. Looking forward to seeing you at the upcoming Business Building Road Show at the LAX Marriott!

This message is jammed full of information and lasts all of about 15 seconds.

When I was carrying the bag, I was known in the region for the quotes I left on my voice mail. I would change them every week and frequently had reps comment that they often called simply to hear the message — which also helped explain the volume of hang-ups!

Wholesalers are supposed to be excellent communicators. Do you leave this obvious tool out of the communication equation?

 ## Is Your Internal Pitch Perfect?

Only 22 pitchers have tossed perfect games in Major League Baseball history.

What about your Internal Wholesaler's pitch?

In a Sunday Night Email, "Defending the Honor of

Wholesaling," I told readers about the advisor I met at a conference who wasn't a fan of too many wholesalers.

Turns out he's an accurate observer and critic of Internal Wholesalers though.

This week, he sent me an MP3 of a message that an internal left for him.

Let's just say it was ... *rough*.

In his email, the advisor commented that it, "Reminded me of a 3 AM infomercial. I thought I was getting pitched a Ronco Rotisserie."

Ouch!

Here's an idea that I successfully used with my internals: simply use your firm's voice mail system to record your pitches for products, sales ideas, etc.

Have your internal listen to these pitches and nail them — just like you present them.

Two voices — one unified message.

Part Three

FOR GREAT WHOLESALERS' EYES ONLY

 ## Laila Wanted Me Fired

When I first started wholesaling, I assumed a territory that had been covered by Gail.

Gail had been with the firm for a long, long time and was good at what she did — in fact, she was a top producer.

She wasn't exactly thrilled that the bank channel had been lifted out from her region and given to me.

Sadly, her lack of enthusiasm for my arrival on her scene was made clear to all, including our clients.

Laila was the manager of a small program that did a fair amount of the firm's business before I arrived.

During my first visit with Laila, I must have said or done something that set her off because she didn't hesitate to call my boss and complain.

Yet, the biggest complaint she had was that I wasn't Gail.

In my next meeting with her I brought up her complaint and the fact that, though I will never be (nor wished to be) Gail, that she should expect great things from our relationship and that I was troubled she thought it appropriate to go to my boss.

And do you know what happened next?

She apologized.

And she admitted that she had no basis, other than Gail leaving, for her complaint.

And that she would like to wipe the slate clean and start fresh.

And so we did.

And every year for seven years, all the folks in her office, including her, were $1-million producers.

Lesson: The right amount of candor, diplomatically dispensed, can often yield unexpectedly terrific results.

Every man takes the limits of his own field of vision for the limits of the world.

— Arthur Schopenhauer

My phone or email in-box receives inquiries about coaching from wholesalers multiple times per week. In the follow-up phone call discussion, my job is to understand the wholesaler's current situation, in what areas of their practice they wish to improve, and why they are exploring the services of a coach.

Over the years, I've heard the same recurring theme during these investigative calls — great wholesalers commit to expending time, money, and a ton of effort on becoming even greater.

They recognize that their field of vision is just that — *their* field of vision — and they seek out ways to improve the periphery of their sight. The improvement may be at the heart of their practice or simply on the margins.

The great wholesalers, and those who aspire to be great, do not confuse their limits with the limits of their craft.

Not Cut Out for Wholesaling

Bad hires.

I've made them, plenty of times.

There was the wholesaler who looked the part in the interview, was dressed to impress, and seemed knowledgeable.

When I went to ride along in the region with him, he arrived with a canvas L.L. Bean bike messenger type briefcase slung over his shoulder.

That first morning of our time together we hailed a cab in NYC, I slid in first, he and his bag followed — spilling coffee from his pre-meeting Starbucks all over my suit.

His brief tenure went downhill from there.

Then there was the wholesaler I hired to work a multi-state region, who I knew was green and trainable.

The problem was he was so afraid of flying that he needed his meds to survive the flight.

I had visions of him nodding off in the advisor's waiting area, drooling on the couch pillows.

He resigned after 90 days.

And to this day my former employees give me a hard time about the Divisional Sales Manager I hired who turned out to be so bad that he was hired and fired in less than 90 days.

Every time a seemingly good hire went bad, I was reminded of the symphony of extraordinary characteristics that truly great wholesalers possess.

Are you one of the great ones?

Tell Me Where It Hurts: Business Planning with Financial Advisors

Are you holding business planning meetings with your best clients?

Plan now to plan for next year.

The end of the calendar year represents an excellent time to have meaningful sit-downs with the top advisors in your region.

This is the time when you will explore what the advisor expects from your partnership and what you need to deliver on.

In return, it represents the best time to get business commitments in plain dollars and cents.

Yes, you need to get those commitments in firm dollars.

Alternatively, you can tell them how much you need from them in order for the partnership to be mutually successful.

On a recent Wholesaler Masterminds Group Call we discussed the importance of "finding out where it hurts."

As you begin your planning session with your clients, think about asking important "where does it hurt" questions. Here are some great examples.

- As you think back on the past year, in what areas did you need your business to improve?

- Are your model portfolios behaving as you had expected?

- Are you net positive or net negative clients versus last year?

- How did the last economic downturn affect your business?

- What product provider changes are you thinking about making in the year ahead? By asset class? By carrier?

- What events do you have planned to reach your existing book of business?

- If you could hire a consultant to help you with one dimension of your business what would that consultant specialize in?

- What are your plans for acquiring new clients?

- Do you have thoughts about integrating social media into your business?

- Who is the best wholesaler who called on you this past year? Why?

All of these questions are designed in some way to get at issues the advisor would rather not talk or even think about. That's why it hurts.

But once you know what ails them, you can begin to prescribe remedies that will deepen the relationships that you have with producers.

Frequently, we offer solutions for pains they don't have.

Or we simply ignore the symptoms they are displaying.

Take the guesswork out — simply ask "where does it hurt?"

 ## The One Question Ticking Off Advisors

What does that advisor think about the job you do?

This past week, a survey went out to financial advisors.

It was written by us.

It was distributed by *Financial Planning* magazine.

The results were both voluminous and telling. And I'm giving you a preview of one of the most frequently commented upon issues that advisors have with us.

This one request that wholesalers make is inflaming the advisor community:

"Tell me about your business," says the wholesaler.

And the advisors in the survey say:

"Don't ask 'tell me about your business.' Know your niche and get to the point quickly."

– Or –

"I hate the 'tell me about your business' question. As with most financial advisors, I'm busy and that question requires too much time."

There are lots more — but suffice to say that we need to do more homework before the meeting and be better informed about the advisor's practice before our butts hit their guest chair.

Advanced Wholesaler Technique: The Benefits of Forward Scheduling

Some skills that wholesalers employ really separate the wheat from the chaff, the posers from the superstars, the men from the … well, you get the idea.

One of those advanced skills is *Forward Scheduling*.

Picture this sequence of events.

- You have a great meeting with a high potential rep. For our purposes, we'll call her The Whale (TW). TW is in your Top 50 for this year and you have every intention of converting her from an occasional seller of your product, better than a one-ticket wonder, to superstar producer status.

- During the meeting you are taking copious notes about where the opportunities lie for both product placement and how to contribute to TW's overall business (yes, I'll even use the "value-added" phrase).

- You now have a number of follow-up items that need to be completed for TW.

  - Putting TW's existing fund grid through an analytics program to test your funds.

  - Running a hypothetical for an immediate income stream for a prospect TW will be seeing.

- Getting information about the availability of a portfolio manager to conduct a call for TW's 20 best clients.

🔳 Before you leave the office you say to TW that in addition to promptly handling the items on the to do list that require immediate follow-up, you would like to schedule the next visit to go through the fund grid and the associated analysis that you will run so you can talk through the results.

🔳 You and TW are now scheduled for four, six or eight weeks out.

🔳 You debrief the visit with your internal and give them the most pressing items on the to do list upon leaving TW's office.

🔳 You put your notes into SalesForce.com (or similar) and …

🔳 *You enter the dates of the next meeting in the forward schedule.*

🔳 Now it's the Internal Wholesaler's opportunity to leverage the benefits of the forward schedule:

- Internal calls TW to follow up on the pressing to do items from the meeting that just took place.
- During the conversation the internal mentions to TW that they see the next appointment on the calendar and that they will be working on the analysis that the wholesaler promised, checking to see that TW doesn't have any additional questions or concerns.

- Internal mentions to TW that they will be back in touch shortly before the next scheduled meeting with the external wholesaler to cover any additional agenda items that TW might like to add.

- A week before the scheduled appointment with TW you send an email to confirm the appointment. Make it short and sweet.

> Whale,
>
> Looking forward to the continuation of our discussion re your practice and how advancing the relationship with Foonman Funds adds to your bottom line.
>
> As a reminder we're meeting on Monday, March 8th at 10:00 AM. If there has been a change to your schedule please let me know as this time is reserved specifically for you.
>
> If there is anything else that you would like me to be prepared to discuss to help you grow your business please let me know.
>
> Regards,
>
> World's Best Wholesaler

To recap, the benefits of Forward Scheduling are:

- Less time spent scheduling, as a number of appointments with your best producers are preset via the last meeting.

- Tighter coordination with your internal partner.

- Keep your rotations/loops in good order.

- Maximize the potential of systems, such as SalesForce.com. If your firm has no such system, simply use a shared Google Calendar.

- Impress reps with your organization skills because most wholesalers simply are not organized.

- Remind reps that you're working on their practice and their agenda (mostly) versus the dreaded "show up and throw up" that too many wholesalers practice.

- Less pressure to fill the calendar the week before a trip.

- Allow your internal partner to help "clear the weeds" before your next in-person visit.

 Lone Wolf Wholesaler

As wholesalers, we often think of ourselves as lone wolves.

We have a reputation for the "leave me alone and just let me produce" type of attitude.

And most wholesalers are just that way — except for the great ones.

The great ones know how to "draft on influentials."

Drafting is defined as "a technique where two vehicles or objects align in a close group reducing the overall effect of drag due to exploiting the lead object's slipstream."

Now think about your firm in its entirety.

Not just the sales department but marketing, legal, product, finance, etc.

How can the folks in these departments help your sales cause?

Do they have connections at accounts where you need to get better traction?

What if you had better alignment with those departments and its employees?

Drawing from the definition above, *you* are the drag.

You cannot get traction at the account or with the advisor.

They are the lead object and provide the slipstream.

They have deep relationships at the account you may not know anything about.

They are the influentials.

You need to be drafting on *them*.

Recently, I was in San Antonio speaking to a group of super talented wholesalers.

The speaker ahead of me was the national sales manager of a mid-sized third party marketer. As a COI (Center of Influence) he was invited to give his perspective to the team. (Note: in the 2011 Winter edition of *I Carry The Bag* we ran a story in which we interviewed COIs.)

In his presentation, he was focusing on the best practices of wholesalers that call on his firm and the areas that are in need of improvement.

His message?

Don't ignore the producers in the middle of the sales pack.

It's what Wholesaler Masterminds call the "Movable Middle."

Many wholesalers focus on two distinct groups: the folks at the top of the sales charts, because everyone wants to bag an Elephant (see "Bud Fox Style Elephant Hunting" later in this section), and those producers who are newer to the firm, in an effort to build allegiances with new arrivals (see "Virgins Wanted" in Part One).

Yet this manager stressed the importance of also focusing on that broad swath of advisors who are firmly placed in the middle.

And we think he is right.

After all, somewhere in the middle is the next Elephant. And doesn't it make sense to have them as a raving fan of you and your firm now, before they blow up, grow tusks, and are impossible to schedule time with?

 One-Hit Wonders

As I built my book of sellers for Oppenheimer Funds, I was tenacious and persistent.

The more a prospect offered resistance, the harder I sold.

Dan was an advisor I called on frequently.

He was a massive producer and wrote almost none of my product.

For years, I diligently called on Dan each time I came through his city.

Each time Dan promised to review the material, present a product, order a hypo — something, anything.

The "competitive me" knew I had to slay this dragon.

Dan was going to be a top producer.

Or not.

After three years of beating my head against the wall (hey, I'm a little slow), I finally cut bait and took Dan out of the rotation — he was wasting my time.

I had allowed the chase of the big producer to cloud my judgment.

Looking back, I know that I let this pattern repeat itself too.

And that's the deceptive sales trap.

Try this as you plan for the year ahead: Go through your list of prospects and one hit wonders and figure out how many you have presented to, followed up with, and heard false promises from.

Then, make a hard and important decision to just stop.

The competitive you will get over the let down.

Your next top producers are just ahead.

And now you'll have more time to devote to them because you're not wasting time.

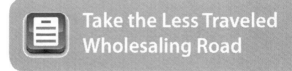
Take the Less Traveled Wholesaling Road

Do you find yourself following in the footsteps of every other wholesaler in your region?

When you have a territory, say, that encompasses Los Angeles, do you find yourself focusing on downtown L.A., the Westside, and the South Bay because that's where all the money allegedly is?

Do you spend all your time in the recognized money centers and related suburbs of Dallas, Chicago, Seattle, New York, Atlanta?

If your time is predominantly spent in offices where every other wholesaler spends their time, what if you took the path less traveled?

What if you went out of your way to spend a portion of your time prospecting for business in less obvious locations, at least less obvious to the masses?

As a wholesaler, I had my best producer located in Redlands, CA. Redlands is some 60 miles due east of Los Angeles and not a place you'd necessarily want to go. But, at one point in my wholesaling career, I had three $2.5 million producers there, one of which was doing between $10M and $12M a year, consistently.

And there were other top producers in places like Libby, MT, and Hilo, HI, and Hanford, CA.

Where in your territory can you find great advisors who do a ton of business, are lower maintenance, and are absolutely delighted that you came to see them?

Versus all the folks that you see in the money centers who simply take you for granted and suck your budget dry.

No, I'm not suggesting that you'll make your annual goal using this method.

Yes, I am saying that you can get a great bump in production by spending a portion of your time prospecting in areas of your region that are on the road less traveled.

 Yes, I Do Windows Too

The things we do to bring in a buck.

An advisor in central California asked me if I would do a seminar for his credit union customers.

As he was a top producer, of course the answer was yes.

After a four-hour drive to Lompoc (yes, it's as out of the way as it sounds) I arrived at the branch.

The first order of business was to set up the room.

Which for most seminars is fairly standard stuff.

Unless it entails moving *all* of the regular branch lobby furniture out of the lobby and replacing it with 100 folding chairs.

Did I mention the part about how the two of us were the only ones doing the set up?

Or the fact that it was in the middle of a summer heat wave?

By the time the seminar attendees arrived I was bathed in sweat.

And, 20 minutes into the presentation the bulb on his projector burned out — and he didn't have a replacement.

Sometimes it's just too glamorous a job — you know?

"We're adding a little something to this month's sales contest. As you all know, first prize is a Cadillac Eldorado. Second prize is a set of steak knives. Third prize is you're fired."

For anyone who has seen *Glengarry Glen Ross*, the classic 1992 film starring a host of acting greats, then you know this quote comes from the amazing seven-minute speech by Blake (Alec Baldwin) as he addresses his underperforming sales team.

And not unlike the group that incurs Blake's wrath, today there are so many wholesalers simply going through the motions.

Blah, blah ... five-year return.

Blah, blah ... out performed in the last market dip.

Blah, blah ... strong renewal rate history.

And then they move on to verbally assault the next warm body while forgetting about or ignoring their ABCs.

Always Be Closing

I talk to wholesalers every day who are just not comfortable asking for the business. For them, and perhaps for you, here are eight ways to move the sales process forward with closes that lead to small commitments, which lead to bigger commitments, which lead to tickets.

1. **Close for an illustration or a hypothetical:** Get a commitment to run a real client scenario that you and/or your internal can revisit and discuss before, or during, your next appointment.

2. **Close for a marketing event:** Seminar, client appreciation dinner, staff training, etc. Let your talent and expertise shine through in one of these venues.

3. **Close for a social outing:** Golf, dinner, ball game, fishing, hunting, quilting (see "23 Client Event Ideas for Wholesalers to Use with Advisors" in Part Two). Find a way to get closer to the rep in question.

4. **Close for a technology lesson:** Take the rep through their proprietary system and show them where to find all the data on your firm and how to process a trade.

5. **Close for a next meeting:** Go back to the beginning of this section and re-read "Advanced Wholesaler Technique: The Benefits of Forward Scheduling."

6. **Close for an at bat:** Ask the rep for a commitment to show your product to a live prospect over the next two weeks and let them know you will be back in touch in two weeks and one day to help answer any questions and/or celebrate their success. Oh, and make damn sure you call on the 15th day.

7. **Close for a ranking in your region:** "Melinda, I'd like to boast to your peers that you are a Top Ten producer for Foonman Funds. My Top Ten starts at $5 million. Are you up to that challenge?"

8. **Close for a firm dollar commitment:** "Vinny, I need you to tell me what our partnership needs to be to earn $1 million from you over the next six months."

Remember that to *Always Be Closing* means that you are seeking out incremental commitments along the sales path that will lead to the objective that you have in mind for that client or prospect.

"Yeah! Woooo! I just bagged the Elephant!" — Bud Fox, *Wall Street* (1987)

Admit it. You have a wee bit of Bud Fox in you.

In the original *Wall Street*, Bud had his sights on the Elephant, Gordon Gekko.

Every wholesaler wants to bag a Gordon Gekko-like Elephant, the huge producer, the corner office king.

Why?

Because an Elephant can single-handedly make your year, catapult you up the production ranking, and make you a hero in your firm damn fast.

One year, I had a producer who got tied into a layoff at a major utility company in Southern California. He was able to position himself in an extraordinary consultative environment as folks were looking for counsel about their retirement plans.

He was a huge producer for me before — that year he became a bona fide Elephant.

$18 million worth of sales in one year.

That's an Elephant in my book, how about yours?

So how will you bag your next Elephant?

In *Wall Street*, Bud befriended Gordon's assistant, brought Cuban cigars, and finally got the meeting.

How are you getting your Elephant's attention to tell your story?

Especially considering that real Elephants are often surrounded by gatekeepers.

They have their screens in place and their defenses up.

Here are some ideas that come to mind.

1. Choose a path to get to the Elephant that is different than the rest of the wholesalers in the great Sea of Sameness. Head to the stationery store (remember those?) and buy some heavy bond, high-end note cards. Use these cards to make your appointment requests in writing.

   Also, choose your delivery method. The card will get noticed. It will get noticed faster if it's FedEx'd. It will get noticed faster still if it's sent via messenger.

2. In my live presentations I discuss the Five New Realities — one of which is that folks don't trust you. It's not personal. The Great Recession has eroded the trust equation. In order to bridge the trust gap faster you need intelligence that will give you a leg up.

   One of the best ways to gather your Elephant intelligence is via Google Reader. As we have discussed before, the useful information you can collect is limitless. If Bud had this technology when he was doing his Gekko homework he would have saved a bunch of time.

3. Use LinkedIn to scope out the points of connectivity you have with the Elephant. Their alma mater, LinkedIn group memberships, former employers, and current contacts all offer clues to ways you might bridge the gap.

4. Facebook offers another set of clues even if you are not friends.

5. Attend the next seminar that the Elephant is hosting. No, don't go as a wholesaler. Go as an interested investor and learn the message and the products that the Elephant promotes.

   Edgier move? Sure — and to bag the big game that's what it may take.

6. Scour the Elephant's website looking for clues. This includes subscribing to the Elephant's newsletter if they have one.

   Implement any of these ideas and you'll be on your way to bagging your next Elephant.

Time to Let a Few "F" Bombs Fly

Sometimes I get a little worked up and need to vent.

Every now and then, I need to let a few choice "F" bombs fly!

Fresh

"Cato said the best way to keep good acts in memory was to refresh them with new." — *Francis Bacon (1561-1626), philosopher*

Have you found new ways to express the same concepts?

When was the last time you overhauled your pitch, training, or product presentation?

Memorability is achieved through variation; the ability to say the same thing in a host of different ways.

Get inside your presentations and find new ways to express your thoughts.

It will increase your MQ — Memorability Quotient®.

Frank

"Who are you and how did you get in here?"

"I'm a locksmith. And, I'm a locksmith." — *Leslie Nielsen (1926-2010), as Lieutenant Frank Drebin, Police Squad!*

More often than not people appreciate the straight truth.

Whether you need to communicate good news (easy) or bad (not easy), give it to them directly.

This does not mean you set tact, empathy, compassion, and understanding aside.

It does mean that you have the unique, memorable ability to share information that others would just as soon skirt around.

Failure

"I succeed because I fail." — *Michael Jordan, NBA star*

We agree that failure rarely (never?) feels good yet there are so many opportunities created from failure.

As an added bonus, failure can sometimes be endearing to a client or prospect.

No, not the "I forgot to place your trade and the market went up 10%" kind of failure.

I am speaking about the small human shortcomings that we all have that are often most memorable.

Your MQ is increased when you allow others to experience doses of your flaws.

Follow Through

"In golf, as in life, it is the follow through that makes the difference." — *Unknown*

How many hollow commitments are made to you each day?

"I'll call you by three."

"The report will on your desk by the end of the day."

"We'll be at your house between one and two on Wednesday."

You can increase your MQ by a substantial amount by simply doing what you say you will do.

Why?

Most folks simply do not.

In an age where commitments are disposable, yours are solid gold.

Funny

"Funny is an attitude." — *Flip Wilson (1933-1998), comedian and actor*

There's a whole lot you could be bummed out about today.

Gas at $3.00 plus.

War. Fires. Unemployment. Real estate values. Recession.

Take that, combined with the fact that we work in the business of caring for people's money — the serious stuff — and you have a recipe for *terminal* seriousness.

Like Flip said, funny is not about wearing lamp shades and pithy one-liners.

What increases your MQ is the ability to find and share humor in the everyday situations, your attitude.

People are more memorable when they use humor to their advantage.

So go right ahead.

Why not let a few "F" bombs fly?

 ## No Means No!

Raise your hand if you have flashbacks to childhood when you hear that phrase.

Maybe that's why I am so vehemently opposed to the word.

So, Thursday nights at Gulfstream restaurant is, as my friend Ray would say, Cougar Night.

We go to be entertained.

Recently, as the server took our order, I asked for a substitution of a side dish that came with the entree.

The answer was, "No."

Remembering my disdain for the word, I went into overcome objection mode.

"Why?" I asked.

"Policy," I was told.

Oh boy, here we go.

The manager was called and the half-hearted/non-sensical case was explained as to why the substitution could not be made.

Remaining calm, I gave my best argument (at this point it was for the sport of it) and was still told that policy prevailed.

Vowing to never return for a meal there (cocktails only and Cougar viewing go together just as well), I completed my order and ate my meal.

Later, the manager returned with a $25 gift card apologizing for the inconvenience.

Was I pleased?

NO!

This was dumb on dumber as far I could determine.

They'd prefer to abide by unintelligible policy and then monetarily apologize, than find a mutually satisfactory outcome to begin with.

Maybe I need therapy.

Great wholesalers deftly navigate the delivery of the word, offer alternatives, and need not offer half-baked, illogical apologies.

How do you handle the "no" when negotiating with financial advisors?

Hold Me Closer, Tony Danza

Admit it.

From time to time, you see a service or product and think, "Why didn't I think of that?"

Examples of this might include the original Smiley Face. For more than 40 years we have all heard the lament from family and friends that this should have been "their" idea.

Here's another one that hit home for me for two reasons — I can't sing and I always screw up the lyrics. Enter the official misheard lyrics book *Hold Me Closer Tony Danza*.

My personal favorite though might well be the Flowbee.

Really, who wouldn't want to cut their own hair, or the hair of a loved one?

And who could pass up the thought of a "refreshing vacuum haircut?"

More recently on a trip to Napa we ran across the same book in almost every winery we visited, *Wine Dogs*.

As the story was told to us by a tasting room employee, whose dog is in the book, about five years ago, a guy came through the valley and started taking pictures of every dog at every vineyard he could find. The dog owners were only too delighted to have their dog featured in the book and the book is now for sale in every single one of those wineries.

Brilliant!

A week after our return from Napa, I find myself not just reflecting on the great wines that we tasted but also further invigorated to continue the pursuit of the innovative endeavors that get the blood juices flowing and have the opportunity to generate more revenue — in part because of *Wine Dogs*.

Whether you work for a small or large firm, the need to innovate, invent, test, trial (all while expecting and learning from the occasional failure) has never been greater.

Why didn't I think of that?

How Valuable Is Candid Feedback?

All faults may be forgiven of him who has perfect candor.
— *Walt Whitman (1819-1892), writer*

Have you ever been asked to give your feedback to a co-worker, employee, or significant other?

If you're like most people, the art of feedback feels more like a chore. As humans, we want to be nice. We don't want to hurt another person's feelings.

By nature we are looking for the bright spot.

So when asked for input most of us will give the softball reply.

"I liked it."

"Nice job."

"You did well."

Part of being truly memorable is helping others through constructive criticism. Our friends, our employees, our co-workers really gain nothing and have no opportunity to grow if we constantly give cream puff feedback.

Without candor, there is no opportunity for improvement.

My wife and I have been together for more than 20 years. She is brutally honest. And each time I ask for feedback and it isn't the kind, complimentary version I was hoping for, I feel hurt ... momentarily. Then after I get off my defensive position, I start to think, to evaluate the merits of these comments. Inevitably I find the hard truth to contain invaluable learning.

As a manager, I have a reputation for being particularly direct.

For employees who are used to spending their careers in exclusively attaboy and attagirl work environments my style takes some folks back a peg or two. It's not that my feedback is focused on the negative. If there are good things to share, I will pile it on high and thick.

It's just that the directness tends to throw folks. They simply are not used to it.

Quickly, they begin to see that my directness is never intended to offend. Rather it is intended to cut through the BS and clutter that they often get and to offer them useful feedback.

Next time you are asked for feedback, why not ask a few qualifying questions about what the recipient wants feedback on? How the report was written? The manner in which the presentation was made? The viability of wearing a hot pink tie?

With that information in mind, you can offer constructive, candid feedback targeted in the direction that is most instructive to the recipient.

While "nice" is ... well ... nice, it does nothing to help friends, colleagues, and employees grow.

Try to dish up some straightforward, honest, well constructed feedback next time you are asked.

It will be received more positively than you might imagine.

 ## Sympathy Is a Wasted Emotion

"Sympathy is a wasted emotion."

Those were the words that I heard from a teacher of psychology many years ago.

What he expressed was that rather than feeling the same emotion as, in our case, a financial advisor, you'd be better served to practice empathy.

Formally the difference is:

sym-pa-thy: feelings of pity and sorrow for someone else's misfortune

em-pa-thy: the ability to understand and share the feelings of another

This memory came alive for me this week while speaking at the Investment Management Consultants Association (IMCA) meeting in Washington, DC, and I entered into a discussion with a high-end advisor.

When I asked him his general opinion about wholesalers his reply was, how shall we say, tepid.

One statement in particular that he made resonated.

He said, "Wholesalers need to remember that they are three emotions removed — they don't have to deal with the end client."

What I heard him saying is that not enough wholesalers demonstrate the qualities that suggest that they truly care about the advisor's business — in this case listening to understand with empathy.

Do you listen simply to find the opening in the verbal joust, only so you can jam the next product idea on the advisor?

Or, do you listen with empathy — a skill set only great wholesalers possess?

Note: Wholesalers — when you are done reading this send it to your boss and your marketing department.

A while ago, I was hosting a Rekon Intelligence event.

For those of you unfamiliar with Rekon, you will be familiar with the set-up — 50 advisors in the room, 7 wholesalers presenting, 30 minutes for each presentation.

Midway through the third presentation, an attendee waived me out of the meeting room.

He then proceeded to blast me with F bombs. I mean his face was red with anger and he was visibly pissed off.

His issue?

Each presenter's slides had data that was presented in 12-point (or smaller?) typeface.

And he, along with more than half of the attendees in the room, was over 50 years of age.

Sure, 12-point type is fine for reading a document in front of your face. But it is unintelligible from two-thirds of the way back in a large meeting room projected onto a screen.

And as the meeting went on, he got more and more dis-engaged.

He tuned the wholesalers out.

Which means the seven wholesalers that presented likely didn't connect with him at all.

Which means they wasted their money and their time being at the meeting.

The winner yesterday was the wholesaler who projected a Form 5500 — Report of Employee Benefit Plan on the screen and cited specific sections — not one of which was readable. (If you're not familiar with a Form 5500, picture a Form 1040 — same tiny type, same fillable boxes.)

Look, I know it's not your fault.

You get the presentation from Marketing with strict orders from Compliance to not change it or they'll string you up from the rafters.

And, just because it's not your fault doesn't mean you are not guilty.

Talk to your boss or the 'marketeers' and let them know that the advisor population — especially the most successful advisors — are not 25 years old.

They are 50, 60, and even 70 years old and (as you younger folks will soon find out) their eyesight just ain't what it used to be.

Alternatively, instead of relying on 12-point type and 10 bullet-point slides, what if you told more stories and relied on PowerPoint less?

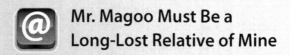

Mr. Magoo Must Be a Long-Lost Relative of Mine

Do you remember the cartoon series *Mr. Magoo?*

For those who don't, via Wikipedia: "Quincy Magoo is a wealthy, short-statured retiree who gets into a series of sticky situations as a result of his nearsightedness, compounded by his stubborn refusal to admit the problem."

Sadly, I can relate.

Except for the part about being short-statured.

Or the part about being wealthy.

But the whole issue about not being able to see worth a damn is spot on.

I used to be able to see anything and everything with crystal clear clarity.

Now?

Well, suffice to say, I have a collection of stylish drug store "readers" in every room of the house and in my car.

Where's this going you ask?

See the previous story.

Wholesaling Chicken or Wholesaling Egg?

I received a question via email that gave me pause for thought. I decided to put it into one of my Sunday Night Emails and ask for reader input.

And input I got!

Here's the question I received:

> I would be interested to hear your thoughts on the following question that I was recently asked in an interview, "Which came first: the relationship or the sale?"
>
> The question came from a sales manager who believes relationships are good but they don't get you the sale.

Really?

My reply was:

> Short answer — relationship.
>
> Period.

If the advisor doesn't connect with you on some level (relationship), there will be no sale.

So I asked readers to let me know what they thought. Can there be a sale without some form of relationship?

Here are a half dozen of the many responses my readers wrote.

1. Many years ago, I had a superb wholesaler who worked for my company. She had no problem getting appointments, and, in fact, led the company in terms of activity. The problem was that there were a lot of meetings, but little in the way of sales! Eventually she reevaluated her business plan and went to those strong "relationships" and said, "Look, I enjoy calling on you and since you always take a meeting with me, you clearly enjoy our interactions. I've noticed, however, that I'm seeing very little business from you. Unless that changes, I'm going to have to stop calling on you and focus my efforts on other financial advisors." Lo and behold, business picked up and she became a top producer! Bottom line is that relationships are important but only to the extent that they can be leveraged and turned into business.

2. While the answer is "yes" there can be a sale without a relationship. But a second sale? Everyone gets lucky but it takes skill to be in this business a long time.

3. I fully agree — relationship first. There are some advisors, however, and to their credit, who won't fully engage in the relationship until they are first investing in your product.

4. The initial relationship is thin, just attraction, bonding, then a small sale to solidify the new relationship. The relationship deepens like a relationship should as two people with a common goal get to know each other. The problem is, most wholesalers take that

first sale and move on, leaving the rest for one of the folks you are coaching!

5. If you make a "sale" without a relationship, consider yourself lucky, but don't expect any repeat business. Unless you have an exclusive on a product that no one else has at a price that no one can match.

6. Relationships come first. Big topic, short answer. I hope this helps.

Are you developing relationships or simply looking for sales?

An old friend, former wholesaler, and current senior leader at a large mutual funds distributor called me today to share a story.

Back in 2003, at a Portland Trail Blazers home game, Natalie Gilbert was called upon to sing the national anthem.

For any 13-year-old young lady, this surely had to have been an honor.

Until it went very wrong.

You see, Natalie, soon after singing the opening lines, froze.

Stiff.

Thank goodness for Mo Cheeks, the then coach of the Trail Blazers.

Mo stepped in, put his arm around Natalie, and encouraged her to continue singing.

While the crowd of 19,980 and he all sang along.

In that moment, Mo Cheeks demonstrated the qualities that advisors will find helpful from great wholesalers in any market.

1. **Support:** Mo was not willing to let this girl fail.

   He took a situation that would have left an indelibly bad mark on her psyche and turned it into a winning moment that endeared both he and Natalie to millions who see their story.

   How supportive are you to the advisors that you serve?

   Do you operate from a position of empathy and support as you work to gain their trust and business?

2. **Encouragement:** Not only did Coach Cheeks lend his support to Natalie, he gave her calm encouragement the whole way through the song.

   He even incited the crowd to join in and sing along louder than they had been singing.

   Advisors also need a bit of cheerleading.

   In an advisor's day that would otherwise be filled with client anxiety and dissatisfaction (even if not directed at the advisor individually), wholesalers have the unique ability to bring an attaboy, a pat on the back, and an encouraging word to the advisor that is slinging their way through the muck of today's market.

3. **Patience:** Mo was not going to let this young girl quit.

   If you watch the video, you'll see that while she really wanted to run and hide, Mo patiently coaxed her along.

   Advisors need your patience.

Many are redefining their business models, asset allocation strategies, and their client's portfolios in the face of a "new normal" that many of us have never before seen or imagined.

4. **Leadership:** Mo stepped up.

   He saw that this girl was about to die a thousand "show biz" deaths and rushed to her aid — unwilling to see her fail.

   You are a leader.

   You have the same ability to step up.

   Lead your advisors through your knowledge and best practices.

Mo Cheeks, beyond his accomplishments on the court, dialed up his MQ — Memorability Quotient® on that day in 2003.

How will you dial up your MQ?

21 Ways Wholesalers Can Shorten the Sales Cycle with Advisors

We've all been there.

One visit leads to five and still not one ticket.

What's a well intentioned wholesaler to do?

Here are 21 ways to shorten the sales cycle.

1. Know the advisor before you visit. Do your homework using the advisor's website, LinkedIn, 411.com, tweepz.com, kgbpeople.com, pipl.com, or zoominfo.com. You can even find out a golfer's handicap and recent round information at the United States Golf Association's Golf Handicap and Information Network (ghin.com).

2. Get referrals from advisors to those prospects that you covet. A referred advisor is 38.6% more likely to do business ... approximately.

3. Be a powerful observer of the contents of the advisor's office. Art work, magazines, awards, photos, etc., all provide clues to knowing the advisor on a different level.

4. Create settings where those advisors who love you are intentionally matched with those advisors who are just "feeling you out."

5. Always lead with the value you provide versus the product that you sell.

6. Represent yourself as a business consultant.

7. Know your product well.

8. Know your competitors' products better than they do.

9. Don't BS your way through an advisor appointment.

10. Have a formal agenda for the advisor appointment.

11. Always have a call to action ready to articulate.

12. Close for something … anything.

13. Have a good sequence of questions to diagnose where the advisor hurts (see "Tell Me Where It Hurts: Business Planning with Financial Advisors" earlier in this section).

14. Always set the follow-up appointment (see "Advanced Wholesaler Technique: The Benefits of Forward Scheduling" earlier in this section) before you leave.

15. Make certain your notes about the meeting are complete and documented for use before the next appointment.

16. Have a systematic follow-up process that clearly delineates what the next steps will be that you and your internal take next to stay in front of the advisor.

17. Book a social event to get the advisor in a setting other than the office.

18. Work COIs (Centers of Influence) for endorsements.

19. Don't neglect COI admin assistants. They often hold the key to the kingdom.

20. Understand that we all learn differently. Have your product pitch consumable in multiple formats, i.e., with product brochure, on a yellow pad, on a computer screen, depending on the rep's preference for how they sell to clients.

21. Teach the advisor how to sell your product. Not just features and benefits — the whole sales story as your most successful producers tell it to their clients.

What are your strategies for shortening the sales cycle?

10 Ways to Ignite the Fuse with a Producer

Every wholesaler that I have ever known has had this dilemma.

Rick was a great prospect. He wrote a terrific amount of over-all business, wrote business in your product wheel house, was open and engaging during the first meeting, worked at a focus firm, placed a literature order with you, and promised to get on board.

And that was as good as Rick was going to get.

He promised a bunch and he was not going to write a ticket.

What are some things that you can do to light the fuse with Rick that will ignite his production?

1. Use your mastery of Forward Scheduling (see "Advanced Wholesaler Technique: The Benefits of Forward Scheduling" earlier in this section) to stay in front of him. If he's a hot prospect, don't let too much time pass, even if your normal rotation has him in an eight-week queue.

2. Get busy with your meeting follow-up.

    - Send a note — handwritten

    - Give your internal partner explicit instructions regarding follow-up — topics as well as time frame

- Phone him back within one week yourself

3. Get Rick engaged in a conversation about a client event. *Any* client event.

4. Start a discussion about a social event with him that plays to *his interests* as you learned via your expert questioning during the initial interview (see "76 Great Questions Wholesalers Should Ask Advisors" in Part One).

5. Start (or add him to) a monthly newsletter list that you send to your VIPs.

6. Put him on your Premier Prospect List (you have one, right?).

7. Invite him to a monthly Producer Business Builder Teleconference that you hold exclusively for your territory.

8. Close Rick for a next action step during the initial meeting: "Do you have enough information about the Foonman Funds' Extraordinarily High Yielding Short Duration Peruvian Government Fund (FFEHYSDPGF), our process, and our returns to present this to three clients over the next week?"

9. Find a Point of Connectivity that you have in common with Rick and leverage it. "Rick, Corner Office Jill, who I know is a mentor of yours, writes a ton of FFEHYSDPGF and speaks highly of our firm."

10. Use a Center of Influence (see "5 Things to Do to Make COIs Love You" in Part Two) to find out more ways to win Rick's business and gain a strategic advantage with Rick.

How do you go about lighting the fuse?

 ## Catsup or Ketchup — It's Still Heinz

On my way back from the gym last week, I was listening to an interview on National Public Radio.

The interviewee, a chef, was answering questions about what's tastier/easier — a homemade product or store bought products.

For example, bacon = store bought (no argument here).

When the chef was asked about ketchup she said, "If it doesn't taste like Heinz, it doesn't taste like ketchup."

She explained that no matter how terrific the homemade version was, the baseline against which it will be measured is Heinz.

So I wondered, how many wholesalers are content to be near imitations of greatness and how many are setting the standard?

Are you Hunt's or Del Monte, constantly chasing from behind, or are you the leader in your market — that others fear and wish to emulate?

What if this is the year you decided to establish your dominance?

What if you decided that this is going to be your Career Year?

3 Ways Wholesalers Can Have More Productive Advisor Meetings

Come on admit it.

We've all done it.

You have every intention of staying on track during that meeting with an advisor and before you know it 30 minutes have gone by in the blink of an eye.

And you were still happily chatting like it was a two-for-one happy hour (see "Run Your Business Like a Business, Not a Clubhouse" in Part One).

You've covered the weather, the playoffs, the family, the dog — and not a word was mentioned about business.

Or worse, your meeting looked like this:

So how can you be better positioned to cover the topics you need to cover, demonstrate your brilliance, and establish your value all in the time allotted?

1. **Time block your meeting agenda.**

   Example for a 30-minute meeting (new prospect):

   0:00 to 0:05 — Random/obligatory chit chat

   0:06 to 0:15 — Meaningful fact finding using your favorite questions from "76 Great Questions Wholesalers Should Ask Advisors" (see Part One)

   0:16 to 0:20 — Clear and concise statement of your PVP — Peerless Value Proposition® (if you don't have one you need to get one) and how it can be applied to the advisor's business

   0:21 to 0:27 — Product pitch

   0:28 to 0:30 — Next steps, forward schedule (see "Advanced Wholesaler Technique: The Benefits of Forward Scheduling" earlier in this section), wrap up.

   Use this as a guideline to formulate your own time block based on your relationship with the advisor, how much time you have been allotted, etc.

2. **Have your agenda (as outlined above) visible to you as you speak to the advisor.**

   This serves a couple of purposes.

   It allows you a better shot at staying on course for the meeting.

Also, the agenda can have reminders on it that only you can see such as "Ask for referrals, dummy!"

3. Send agendas in advance of the meeting.

One of our favorites.

Along with your confirmation email of the appointment, you send a quick and dirty agenda that points out the high level items you'll be discussing with the advisor during your meeting.

And then you add the most important line:

Please email me back to let me know of any specific agenda items you'd like for me to address when we meet.

You have now allowed yourself to diffuse any issues in advance (product or service concerns, for example) and be prepared to meet the advisor's expectations for the meeting — assuming they have any.

How productive are your advisor meetings?

Part Four

WILL YOU SURVIVE THE WHOLESALING MARATHON?

 Are You an Automatic?

In the early 1980s, I helped establish an executive search firm in Los Angeles.

As a start-up, our goal was to be considered alongside of the big players when an employer needed staffing in the LA financial services community.

Years later, this concept took a larger stage as I traveled around eight western states developing business for a (then) small, lesser-known mutual fund provider.

Our goal in the region was to become an "Automatic."

Our aspiration was to not allow a financial advisor in the midst of a product line-up decision to finalize her decision without speaking to us.

We knew if we had the chance to be in the beauty pageant, there was a high likelihood we would win it.

Think about it this way: if you are looking to buy an economical car from a foreign manufacturer, you most likely will not buy until you check out a Honda.

What makes Honda or you an Automatic?

Three key ingredients:

1. Relentless execution: doing the right things over and over again.

2. Earned reputation: making certain that everything that you do every day is mindful of, and accretive to, your reputation.

3. Advocates aplenty: using the right fertilizer to grow a deep and passionate fan base.

So, are you an Automatic?

I n the Introduction to this book, I mentioned the interview in which I was asked if I understood that Oppenheimer-Funds would own me Monday through Friday. That was my first clue that the profession we are in is a *lifestyle* not a j-o-b.

And, unlike a car salesperson, we can't see tangible results of our sales efforts in the form of Mr. and Mrs. Farquart riding off in their shiny new Honda.

So our jobs are marked by a series of activities and behaviors that need to be crafted, tested, honed, and repeated multiple times throughout our careers.

The fact is that our wholesaling careers are a marathon race, and whether you are at mile marker 4 or mile marker 24, you'll need to check in with some wisdom that will help you finish the race without having a heart attack along the route.

This section is dedicated to giving you the benefit of the collected wisdom of your peers; wisdom that is drawn from experience along with years of trial and error.

 The Wholesaling Marathon

Valuable lessons.

We've all learned them.

Back at the beginning of my wholesaling career there was a manager (Anne) who asked if I could do a meeting on a Friday.

My (dumbest possible) answer was, "Fridays are my office days. I don't do appointments."

As I was new on her wholesaling scene, Anne decided to call my boss and vent her displeasure with my answer.

Thankfully, rather than ripping me a new one, my boss explained that Anne had a history of volatility.

And then she said something that resonated loudly.

"Build the best relationship with Anne that you can … and, the fact is, you will outlast her in this business."

Whoa!

Sound advice.

Sure enough, less than a year later, Anne was gone — and did not resurface in my wholesaling world.

She was built to run a 100-meter race.

I was learning to run the marathon called wholesaling.

How's your race being run?

A Lot More than 10 Rules for Wholesalers

The wisdom of our elders.

I was speaking at the Center for Due Diligence conference (CFDD) in Chicago and was introduced to a long tenured wholesaler.

He's been around so long that telephones with a dial (versus crank) had just come into vogue when he started his career!!

As we spoke over an adult beverage he told me he had *10 Rules of Wholesaling*.

I insisted that he share them with me so I could share them with you.

Here they are — in the exact format I received them:

#1 DON'T WHOLESALE DURING FAMILY TIME!!!!! (on vacation, etc.)

#2 Don't spend ANY time dissing the competition. NADA.

#3 Don't eat alone (makes you look like a loser).

#4 Don't swear — no matter how much you want to. No F bombs.

#5 Send your expense account weekly. Absolutely NO padding.

#6 Keep your car clean.

#7 NEVER TELL ANOTHER ADVISOR WHAT YOU ARE WORKING ON.

#8 Be discreet and moderate at ALL company sales meetings.

#9 Treat your internal with respect, kindness and professionalism.

#10 NEVER tell anyone how much you earn. Never. Ever.

Once I shared this with my Sunday Night Email readers and folks started sending in additions to put on the list — some similar, some new, all good, and all appreciated.

- Limit your drinking to one or two drinks with advisors, home office, and colleagues. Stay in control at all times.

- If you don't have an answer to an advisor's question, say, "That's a great question and at this time I do not have the answer. I will have it for you by the end of day/close of business tomorrow."

- Don't drive a flashy car. At one point in my career I was an advisor and I remember seeing a wholesaler driving an Audi A8, then later that week I saw another driving a Toyota Camry. All things being equal investment-wise and I liked them both, I gave my business to the Camry guy because I figured the A8 guy was doing just fine.

- Never, and I mean *never*, complain about your compensation being down compared to last year. It has been really tough on advisors these past few years and they do not want to hear about how you use to make $500k but now only make $400k. This will fall on deaf ears and create resentment.

- Shine your shoes.

- Never, ever, never date the assistant.

- Build on a personal brand — you are what makes the difference.

- Always follow up on requests with a personal note or call to make sure the request was fulfilled.

- Listen to what your clients want and give them the best that you can.

- Walk in your clients' shoes and know their challenges.

- Your clients will have good and bad days but you can only let them see your great days.

- Never cancel a meeting (unless illness or emergency).

- Never be late to a meeting.

- If you are late — call yourself; it's better than your internal doing it.

- Get to know the assistant.

- Be good to the receptionist. Once you know the gatekeepers, getting a meeting is pretty straight-forward.

- Introduce yourself to the branch manager, out of respect for his position.

What wholesaling rules would you add to this list?

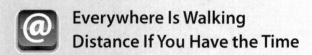

Everywhere Is Walking Distance If You Have the Time

"Everywhere is walking distance if you have the time."
— *Steven Wright, (1955-), comedian*

It's all about perspective, isn't it?

Sometimes we need someone with a completely different view of the world to reframe our thoughts.

One time my assistant got a call from one of our wholesalers, who had received a call from our corporate credit card company, telling her that her stolen credit card had been found.

On a dead body!

Without blinking an eye, the assistant commented, "That's good; at least the card hasn't been used yet."

Next time you are staring down into the vortex of wholesaling insanity, go seek out someone with an alternative thought process to rearrange your perspective.

Wholesalers: What Style of Communicator Is Your Sales Manager?

On a recent Wholesaler Masterminds call, the group and I were discussing the best ways to build a successful relationship with and leverage the talents of your immediate manager.

One participant suggested that in order to communicate most effectively with the manager a wholesaler should understand and implement the manager's preferred style of communication.

- **The live and in person manager:** While somewhat of a throwback to days gone by, and obviously out of place in a fast moving world of instant communication, this manager only wants to have conversations face to face. They have less ability to connect via phone and almost no ability to connect via email. As a wholesaler this is hands down the hardest manager to communicate with.

- **The live on the phone manager:** Managers in this category, like the one above, have not found a comfortable place with instant forms of communication and are infinitely more effective in a live phone discussion. This means that they may take longer to connect with you, depending on conflicting schedules.

Conversely, you'll often have interactions that go deeper than:

- **The email or text addict manager:** He or she only gives you short blasts of one- to two-sentence texts that at first appear curt and impersonal. That said, this manager will likely be the first to respond. Although, you might need to decode the response — requiring a live conversation.

- **The voice mail manager:** Perhaps the easiest manager for the wholesaler on the go to communicate with as you don't need super-human "read between the lines" skills as with the email/text addict. You get to hear voice inflection, volume, pace, and use those to add more texture to the communication.

Obviously, there is no one style of communication that makes for the ideal wholesaler-manager relationship and all four of these forms of communication have their appropriate place.

Yet often by learning, acknowledging, and utilizing your manager's preferred style of communication, you will develop better dialog, get issues resolved faster, and provide a more satisfying experience for both parties.

If this sounds too basic then why are so many wholesalers so frustrated with their manager's communication?

Sushi, Sake, See Ya!

If I was dying, and granted a last meal, a juicy steak would be tempting, but I'm certain that my choice for a last meal would be sushi. Ever since my introduction to sushi in 1978, we have had a deep and meaningful relationship.

During the early 2000s, my favorite hangout was a local place in Dana Point called Gen Kai. I was so smitten with this particular sushi bar that I leapt at any reason to eat there.

Saturday date night? Gen Kai.

Relatives in town? Gen Kai.

Client dinner? Gen Kai.

And so it was that when my boss came to town, my first suggestion for dinner was my favorite sushi bar.

It also provided the backdrop for one of the most important management lessons I have ever learned.

As we made our way through the omakase (chef's choice) morsels and washed the bites down with premium sake, my boss spoke about his visits to my territory.

"Shoot, I like coming out here (from NY) just to see you and eat great sushi," he said.

"What I like best is that we can just do this great dinner, I can tell you what a great job you are doing, and then I can move on."

At that moment I was flattered, feeling that I did not need his counsel anyway.

Fortunately, I was doing a great job and had been number one in my division for over three years. My territory had grown from eight western states to only Southern California. I enjoyed #1 or #2 market share at every account I served.

My boss was validating all the things I knew to be true about my production and current position at the firm.

And that was the problem.

He fell into the same trap that so many managers fall into.

He did not want to rock a top producer's boat. He likely felt that any constructive criticism would have been received badly. He may have thought that a candid critique, if taken the wrong way, might lead to my departure.

Yet being a top producer didn't mean I knew it all, had the job wired, or couldn't benefit from his guidance.

Over the years, I have seen other managers make the same mistake, sometimes with disastrous consequences.

For example, there was the manager who overlooked the "quirks" of an advisor (now banned) who consistently grossed $60,000 per month, only to find out he was billing multiple fund companies for the same event expenses. Or that he had a reputation for "dating" staff at his office.

The manager was afraid to rock the boat. Sadly, the NASD rocked his world for failure to supervise.

What's your role as a manager to your top producers? Are you an ego-stroker? A glad-handing back-slapper?

Or are you a manager who doles out healthy portions of top producer praise while, at the same time, finding ways to add constructive value to the care, feeding, and development of that top producer?

Upon reflection, the dinners that I shared with my boss at Gen Kai would have had a longer-lasting impact, and more meaning, had he chosen to coach me — not simply praise me.

Some Wholesalers Are Like Stale Real Estate Listings

Are you gunning for a promotion?

Perhaps you are an internal who desperately wants to get to the outside.

Maybe you're an external who wants to get into management.

How about a divisional who has his sights set on senior management?

You've put your name in the hat for the job you want and have been rejected repeatedly.

You, my friend, have become like the house in my neighborhood that has been on the market for the last 782 days.

You have become stale.

And, like a stale home that needs to be sold, what's the best thing to do?

Take it off the market!

Then, perform an inventory of all of the issues that are preventing it from being sold such as:

- Inspect the overall appearance
- Tune up the curb appeal
- Add some interior staging

- Recheck the comparables for proper pricing
- Re-evaluate the marketing approach

Only then can you relist the home and reinvigorate the pool of prospective buyers.

If you have found yourself being rejected repeatedly for the position that you covet, you need to take yourself off the market and perform an inventory of all of the things that are standing in the way of your dream job.

These might include:

- Your professional appearance and/or demeanor (or lack thereof)
- Your presentation skills
- How you navigate the political waters of your firm
- How you build relationships with advisors (see "4 Things Advisors Need from Wholesalers in Challenging Markets" in Part Three)
- How you build relationships with COIs (see "8 Ways Wholesalers Succeed with COIs" in Part One)
- How you build relationships with home office staff (see "14 Guaranteed Ways to Achieve Success with Your Internal Wholesaler" in Part One)
- Your ability to manage a budget
- Your ability to manage up
- Your overall communication ability (email, voice mail, in person)

Remember:

"Insanity: doing the same thing over and over again and expecting different results." — *Albert Einstein (1879-1955)*

 The Croissant

There it sat in the display case in all of its golden, glistening, light, flaky goodness.

The light from the pristinely clean glass was illuminating my craving, making it irresistible.

While the angel on one shoulder was saying, "Don't do it," the devil in me was screaming, "Just eat it!"

So I caved and ordered the croissant.

As I tore off a piece, I anticipated the melt-in-your-mouth flavor.

And as I bit down I almost chipped a tooth.

Yep, stale.

Hard. As. A. Rock.

It's kind of like wholesaling.

Just because you wear a $1,000 suit, carry a Tumi bag, and look great on the outside doesn't mean that your skills — after many years in the field — haven't become stale.

I remember speaking to a crazy successful wholesaler (a seven-figure guy) who was exploring coaching because he was concerned about that very fact.

He was looking to have a Career Year.

Are you?

Confessions of a Wholesaling Workaholic

Guilty as charged — and that's all I have to say.

Work consumes who I am.

It defines my existence.

And I am not proud of this fact.

And I'm damn sure not alone, especially in our business.

You get paid a ton of money relative to other professions and you work endlessly.

How many family life events have you missed?

I remember one time I was away for my wife's birthday and my boss called to apologize to *her* that his meeting conflicted with her celebration.

During my coaching sessions I have heard about breakups, divorces, missed kid's soccer championships, missed school parent-teacher conferences, etc., etc.

I've worked with folks who are consumed by dragging the rock around that says, "My call reports are not done for the last month and my boss is pissed."

Hell, I know of wholesalers who are paralyzed by the anxiety that is created by the weight of six weeks of unattended expense reports.

The reality is much of this comes with the turf. It's part of the price you pay.

Look, we both know that wholesaling is a lifestyle. It's not just a j-o-b.

But can you learn how to add more balance to your work/life equation?

Yes.

Some of you might not need the whole "balance" thing attended to.

And some of you are kidding yourselves if you think you don't.

 Time to Do My Nails

I've admitted it before, I'll admit it again: I tend to be a workaholic.

And no, it's not something I'm proud of.

One time I had a key account manager come out to my region from New York, and before her arrival, I shared with her a list of local target firms I was trying to get selling agreements with — assuming she would reach out to them during her visit.

After connecting with her by phone the morning she landed in Los Angeles, we agreed that she would meet me at a seminar where I was speaking later that night.

Upon arriving at the seminar, I excitedly asked how her visits with our clients *and my target firms* went.

She matter-of-factly and somewhat indignantly replied, "Huh? I got a manicure!"

Lesson #1: She was not a workaholic.

Lesson #2: Assume nothing.

The One About the Spineless Wholesaler

Too many wholesalers are spineless.

There, I said it.

How often has this scenario happened to you?

Danny Supernova is an advisor whom you drool over.

He and his team have over $500 million under management and you know they are writing your niche of product — they are just not writing your product.

After the initial visit Mr. Supernova intimates that there may be some business for you on the horizon *if* …

If you provide the office with a "lunch and learn" — oh, and please go easy on the learn.

If you pony up $1,000 for his upcoming client event — on the boat, with the bartender, and the catered food, with the band.

If you arrange for he and his lead Portfolio Analyst to have a call with your lead Portfolio Manager on the product he thinks he might use.

And so you start the dance.

Lunch scheduled — check.

$1,000 contribution to the client event — check.

Conference call with PM — check.

And then you wait for the tickets to start rolling in.

Except they don't.

And the next time you try for an appointment, Mr. Supernova's calendar is booked, so says his assistant.

And the voice mails that you leave for Mr. Supernova are, as yet, unreturned.

The question is: What do you do now?

Too many wholesalers I speak with today, or have managed in the past, simply move on to the next prospect and never resolve the issue.

And that's too bad because every one of these wholesalers, when pressed, feels horrible about being "had" and wasting company resources — never mind their own time.

So what would you do to get this resolved in a manner that, at a minimum, provides you with clear answers?

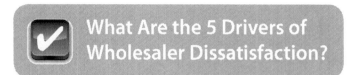
What Are the 5 Drivers of Wholesaler Dissatisfaction?

Unique to the profession, wholesalers frequently spend hours upon hours alone. They are driving long distances from point A to point B, enduring unending air travel delays, or are holed up in the local Hilton.

And, not at all unique to the profession, during that alone time they have time to think.

Sometimes as they think they become increasingly dissatisfied.

And like listening to a dripping faucet in a rundown Radisson, they get obsessed by the noise of their thoughts.

So what is it that wholesalers are dissatisfied about?

1. **Lack of communication:** The marketers in the firm, working alongside of senior management, have crafted a new incentive program, or perhaps operations had to send a recovery notice to public customers, or maybe it was simply a state of the union letter from the firm's CEO sent to producers.

   In all three cases the communication did not reach the wholesaler before the intended recipient.

   And in all three cases the wholesaler got blindsided by questions about something they knew nothing about.

Managers, let your partner departments know that you have a "central clearing house" for all important communications and you'll distribute on their behalf.

Granted, you can lead a wholesaler to the memo, but you can't make them read … and that's a topic for another column.

2. **The missing layer of management:** The financial meltdown caused historic layoffs in our business. Among those laid off were a small army of middle managers.

   Whereas prior to the meltdown, Divisional Managers had 10-12 direct reports, today it is not uncommon for managers to have 15+ wholesalers — in addition to serving another role of, say, National Sales Manager.

   The results are frequently not pretty.

   Longer response time on escalated items, over-whelmed managers missing email messages, and the general inability to touch the folks that need frequent touching — wholesalers.

   As one client stated, "Try as I might there is no way to keep up with literally the hundreds of emails that hit my screen every day."

   The result is that wholesalers can get the impression, albeit wrongly, that management does not care or is not operating with the right sense of urgency.

3. **"Don't mess with my money:"** That was a direct quote from another client. In this case the wholesaler was lamenting accounting failures that caused his

commission checks to be wrong — multiple months in a row.

As important to the correctness of the calculation and issuance of timely checks, so too is the recovery if the process breaks down.

"We'll pay you next month" is perceived to mean "management doesn't give a rip."

"We'll correct the problem and FedEx an out-of-cycle check" is interpreted as "Hey, things happen and I appreciate you making good."

The kissing cousin to this has similar effects on wholesalers: mid-year compensation changes. Most wholesalers are programmed to know that all compensation bets are off starting January of any new year. It's the mid-year changes that cause the most discontent.

4. **Things that fall out of the ivory tower:** A national sales manager recently told me that his firm vets all new producer marketing materials, seminars, consumer brochures, etc., through a group of wholesalers to make sure their voice is heard.

   He then told me that the firm enjoys high wholesaler retention and that the average tenure of his team is seven plus years.

   Coincidence?

   Not a chance.

   Wholesalers frequently bemoan the fact that their voices are not heard. That new programs, processes, and protocols simply fall out of the ivory tower and those in charge do little to cushion the fall.

5. **Operations not operating:** A wholesaler schedules an appointment with a producer for three weeks out. Prior to the meeting the Internal Wholesaler does a great intro call and the producer writes their first ticket.

    Upon walking into the rep's office the wholesaler is presented with three confirm statements that have the client's name spelled incorrectly and that reflect the wrong social security number. Seems that the advisor's assistant tried to get the matter corrected with Operations and had no success — three times!

    A great wholesaler visit to potentially catapult a new producer to top producer status turns into an unfortunate distraction and annoyance.

    When it happens four more times that month it becomes a bona fide measure of wholesaler dissatisfaction.

Each of these five examples is culled from the living archive of my conversations with wholesalers every day. While they recognize that to have a job in the post meltdown world is something to be thankful for, they also know that the clouds are parting.

Firms that choose to not recognize these signature signs run the risk of finding themselves in precarious straits as the employer job market of today morphs into the employee job market of the post-recession tomorrow.

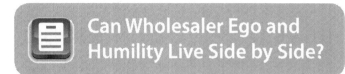
Can Wholesaler Ego and Humility Live Side by Side?

We work in an industry that is filled with egos.

Big egos.

Hell, one of my favorite quotes comes from a pin that was given to me by a co-worker when I was all of 20 years old in my first financial services job.

The pin said, "Where ego I go too."

For wholesalers ego is, in part, a survival skill because wholesalers dine on rejection every day.

It's also bred by the incomes our business affords.

After all, there are not many other industries where marginal producers have the ability to make $250,000 per year.

Yet many wholesalers are confused.

They mistakenly believe that their over-the-top swagger, self-aggrandizing behavior and in-your-face pretentiousness is a winning formula for long-term success.

Here is the secret that great wholesalers find out as they mature.

Ego and humility can comfortably live side by side.

You can still be humble and have an ego — or a presence that doesn't demand outrageous ego tactics.

Quietly confident wholesalers have a magnetic quality.

Out of control, outrageously egotistical wholesalers can reek like a bad case of body odor.

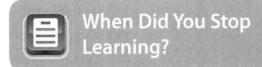
Recently, I had lunch with my friend, Mike. His brother "Jake" sells commercial insurance. He has created a focused and tight niche directed at commercial divers. Guys and gals who weld things like gas lines in the middle of the ocean.

It seems that Jake has made quite a name for himself in his niche. He has found a way to go directly to the underwriting insurance company and skip the traditional intermediate brokerage relationship.

One day Jake received a call from one of the legacy brokers in this particular area. In fact, this broker had dominated the market for more than 30 years — until now.

During the conversation, the broker asked in amazement how Jake got access to the niche. How did he locate his prospects? How did he get direct access to the carrier without a broker intermediary?

Jake explained that he does relentless research. He spends unfathomable amounts of time dialing in the answers to these questions and dozens more. In short, he became a recognized expert and trusted source of this highly specialized insurance product — and in the process boxed out the legacy broker from a ton of business.

Then Jake asked the 60-year-old broker one gutsy, but honest, question, "When did you stop learning?"

Are you still learning?

Do you devote Jake-like time to getting deep in the weeds of your craft?

In the absence of what I have always referred to as "student of the business" learning, you, or your sales force, are at risk.

At risk of finding out that another sales team or individual sales professional has figured out a way to reengineer the system.

At risk of realizing that your "standard operating procedure" is now an antiquated approach.

At risk of losing market share, revenue, and profits.

Take a good look around your shop and in the mirror. You haven't stopped learning, have you?

 ## The Powder Blue Wall Phone

How can you tell the real age of a house you want to buy?

Not the year it was built, because it might have been improved, but the real age.

In the case of the house that The Mrs. and I have made an offer on there is one telling giveaway.

While the real estate agent is doing her best to sell the idea that it needs "a coat of paint and new carpet," we noticed something else.

It was indicative of the fact that the house had not been updated in any way, shape, fashion, or form in a long time — if ever.

While looking at the kitchen, once we got past the dated appliances, we noticed that there was a powder blue telephone mounted on the wall.

Not only that, it was a powder blue wall phone with a rotary dial!

Hello 1972.

The house is a lot like wholesalers who fall into a state of disrepair, neglect their practice and/or fail to upgrade to the latest technology.

How about you?

Any signs of powder blue rotary wall phones in your practice?

Good News! I Got Fired and I'm Leaving Wholesaling

The Monday after Christmas I had a private coaching call scheduled with one of my Wholesaler Masterminds participants. I was looking forward to this call as Hal (not his real name) was a newer wholesaler (less than three years' experience) and has worked at a firm that has had senior level management shake-ups and dubious local management support. I knew from our group calls that there was a great deal to discuss and felt confident that I could make a difference.

As we got past the holiday niceties and into the purpose of the call, Hal takes a sharp left turn and explains that he received a call just prior to Christmas and was no longer with the firm. In addition, he explained that a huge weight felt like it had been removed from his shoulders and that he was done with wholesaling.

As a devotee of our profession, I felt a bit deflated and disappointed.

Hal explained that after trying to get airtime with advisors for a less well known company, enduring three strategy shifts at the firm courtesy of multiple C-suite changes, and dealing with a Divisional Manager who, in his opinion, was clueless, he was done with the whole financial services wholesaling thing.

And then I started thinking about the fact that it is true enough that not everyone is cut out for this line of work. After all, the hours are longer than long, the role we play in advisors' lives ranges from teacher to minister to pseudo-friend, and the job is flat-out hard.

Unfortunately, Hal had those other headwinds that made it even harder.

Working for a boss who adds no value to your career evolution is certainly frustrating. Wholesalers should have a manager who makes their jobs easier and helps propel their careers.

Watching the guy in the first chair at the firm change multiple times in only five years is indeed frustrating. Getting on board with a new set of directives, strategies, and tactics can be tiring.

Hawking a product that few are familiar with has great challenges. And yet not every wholesaler gets to show a name brand product — and that name brand product may not even be the best solution.

Hal did try. I had to give him that. He reached out and sought coaching — and paid for it out of pocket. That alone speaks volumes to me.

Yet, I can't help but believe that Hal made a mistake.

I know it's his career to manage but won't the challenges be the same in pharmaceutical sales, for example?

It's another highly regulated industry with razor thin margins.

Sales managers in that industry are, after all, still sales managers.

Your drug versus the other firm's drug.

Great doctors to call on and doctors you would like to report for malpractice.

Wholesaling is one of the truly great professions. While not for everyone, it has a great combination of "assisted entrepreneurialism," extraordinary earning opportunity, and the ability to make a difference in the lives of those who use our products.

Did Hal make a mistake by leaving our business?

That's Hal's question to answer.

 3 Questions to Ask Yourself

I've asked my coaching clients the following three questions recently:

1. As a wholesaler, what one trait/characteristic are you most proud to display to clients and prospects?

2. What one flaw do you hope they will never see?

3. What is the one change that you could make to your process, presentations, relationships,

prospecting, organizational skills that would
catapult you to the next level of desired success?

Think about how you would answer them — and
more importantly what have you done to exploit,
address, or remedy each of these?

1. What skills will it take to achieve your best year yet — your Career Year?

2. Do you have the business plan that will get you there — and do you refer to that plan throughout the year?

3. Are your rotations solid, sustainable, and well disciplined?

4. Have you considered the SWOT (Strengths, Weaknesses, Opportunities, and Threat Analysis) analysis of your territory and how you'll respond to each component?

5. Is the relationship you have with your Internal Wholesaler positioning you for a Career Year? (See "14 Guaranteed Ways to Achieve Success with Your Internal Wholesaler" in Part One.)

6. What support are you getting from your boss — and have you asked for the assistance that you need to achieve your Career Year goal?

7. Do you position yourself the proper way in your region to establish your dominance?

8. Can you articulate your PVP — Peerless Value Proposition® to both clients and prospects alike?

9. Are your closing skills getting you business? (See "Great Wholesalers: 8 Ways to Always Be Closing" in Part Three.)

10. How do you stay fresh after five, seven, ten, twenty years of carrying the bag?

11. Can you describe your systematized follow-up process?

12. Do you set quarterly goals and review them at the end of each quarter?

13. Are you becoming a wholesaling robotron?

14. What kind of manager/team leader are you?

15. How good is your time management?

16. Is creativity a strong suit for you or are you perpetually stuck in the left brain?

17. Have you established a solid mentor relationship?

18. Do you run your business like a business? (See "Run Your Business Like a Business, Not a Clubhouse" in Part One.)

19. Are you truly motivated to succeed in the coming year?

20. Who holds you accountable for the commitments you make and the activities that you undertake?

Are you on your way to a Career Year?

11 Things Wholesalers Must Do to Ensure a Long and Successful Career

At a recent conference I met a long tenured wholesaler who spoke about a list he created that defined the ten things wholesalers must do to ensure a long and prosperous career.

Of course I asked him for the list.

That led to the Sunday Night Email, "A Lot More than 10 Rules for Wholesalers" (earlier in this section).

And, after almost 25 years in wholesaling/distribution, I thought I'd create a list of my own.

1. **Get your priorities straight.**

   I've said it before and I'll say it again, if you are not vigilant this job will own you.

   Knowing that, you had better make up your mind that family, friends, health, and pursuits beyond wholesaling are critically important.

   They are the nutrients that feed your career and your life.

   They allow you to do what the job requires at the highest level necessary.

   Without them you will find yourself hollow.

   Don't screw this up.

2. You are not that important.

At a recent speaking engagement at a wholesaler meeting I was talking with a National Sales Manager who related his experience at the Human Performance Institute.

Upon arrival, the program facilitators collected his cell phone and told him he would not get it back until after the two-day session was completed.

"You are not that important," they reminded him.

The business will go on.

To this day he turns off his smartphone late Friday night and doesn't turn it back on until Sunday night.

3. Kiss your spouse and babies.

Wife, husband, girlfriend, boyfriend, kids, dogs, cats, goldfish — it doesn't matter.

You likely have a propensity to neglect the ones you love.

I have one client who hired me to focus her on making sure she was able to enjoy the 90 days of maternity leave she was about to experience without caving in to the demands and temptations of voice mail, email, sales reports, and sales rankings.

This means that you no longer sit in the driveway on the phone while kids and dogs anxiously await you crossing the front door threshold — 30 minutes later.

Your career will be significantly crappier if you screw up your most important relationships.

4. **Be mindful of the excesses of the job.**

   You probably have an ample expense account that affords both the opportunity and the mandate to entertain.

   And if you are not careful, that combination can lead to behavior that you later may not be proud of.

   Many years ago there was a wholesaler who, while attempting to be the life of the bar party, thought it would be entertaining to demonstrate the explosive nature of human flatulence and fire.

   He was fired and has not been heard from since.

5. **Carefully navigate your ethical boundaries.**

   If you have not been tempted by, or acted upon, a top producer's outrageous request, you will be.

   It will come in the form of that event or financial request that your inner voice says, "This is shady, and I likely shouldn't be doing it."

   Listen to that inner voice.

   There are unemployed wholesalers aplenty who caved to outrageous requests in pursuit of the large trade — only to run afoul of compliance or FINRA (Financial Industry Regulatory Authority). The income and freedom that your position affords are unique in the financial services industry.

   Don't believe me?

   Just ask one of the hundreds (thousands?) of folks who have been evicted from the business since 2008.

6. Guard your brand.

You are the brand.

Yes, you carry the products and business cards of great firms.

Yet, at day's end, it's you and your reputation.

Filter your decisions accordingly. If you wish it to be, it can be a long and highly rewarding career.

7. It's not always greener grass — it might be crab grass.

Yes, you are tempted to test the free agent employment waters.

After all, even in a sketchy economy, superstars are rewarded handsomely.

And yet there are countless wholesalers who lament that the "evil" they knew was better than the one they just met.

Think twice before making a job change.

Besides, there are only so many times you can show up in a producer's office with another business card from a new firm before they know that you are a job-hopping flake.

8. Management isn't a natural next stop on the career train.

Yes, you have been a wholesaling ninja.

No, that doesn't mean that you'll be a good manager.

The skills and politics of management require a whole different tool box.

It's a gig that may look tasty from far away, but if not done right will leave a very bad taste once you are fully engaged.

Do your homework about the demands and pitfalls of management *before* you raise your hand for the next promotion.

9. **Beware the "freshman 15" and its kissing cousin "you've train wrecked your health and now you're screwed."**

It's one thing to enjoy the perks and opportunities of wholesaling (read: expense account lunches, dinners, lavish events, etc.).

It's another to not wake up and smell the scent of excessive fat and ill health.

Recently, I learned of a wholesaler, in his early 40s, who simply keeled over one day and died.

Do I have the first clue as to what his diet or genetics were?

No.

What I do know is that the obesity epidemic that faces our country hasn't skipped over the wholesaling community.

Do yourself, and the folks that depend on you, a favor. Examine what you are putting in your mouth.

Commit to some regular exercise — *any* regular exercise.

10. Stay humble and pick your battles.

Cocky and arrogant is not attractive.

So why is it that many of our peers show off this trait like it's the latest NYC Fashion Week style?

It's far more satisfying to be confident in yourself knowing that you have no need to endlessly prove your point.

It's also wisest to take a stand only when the stand you wish to take is the one you really want to fall on your sword for.

Otherwise you'll get labeled as a "whiner."

And that's a label you don't need nor want.

11. Manage you own money wisely.

What a great business we are in.

We make more than 90% of the wage earners in America.

We also speak to people all day about prudent investing.

So why is it that too many wholesalers are over-extended and stretched beyond their means?

Let me be the one to remind you — pay yourself first.

Get out of debt.

Amass a chunk of money — or as many like to call it "f&%k you" money — that will allow you to have far less pressure next time the winds of change and retrenchment blow over our industry.

This isn't a complete list — simply one derived from personal experience and observation.

Are your actions and behaviors aligned to provide a long and successful career?

 Pool Man Jumped the Shark, So I Fired Him

Like many Southern Californians, there is water in my backyard — an in-ground spa.

It's small enough to care for myself, yet large enough that I don't want to.

Enter: Terry the Pool Man.

During his pitch to get the job, Pool Man outlined all of the services he would perform on each visit.

He prided himself on his ability to do the job more knowledgeably, consistently, and reliably than his competition.

For the first year, his weekly service was quite good.

And then things changed.

He started to skip weeks — and charge me for them.

Pool Man was hired to check chemicals, empty filter baskets, sweep, and vacuum.

Over time, one or more of these items was not performed with each visit as promised.

Pool Man's reliability decreased and his excuses increased.

Finally, after three weeks of no show, no email, no call, no nothing, Pool Man was fired.

He started taking my business and loyalty for granted.

A promise of consistency translated over time into haphazardness.

A promise of reliability deteriorated into unpredictability.

Pool Man had jumped the shark.

He was now in decline.

What about your business?

As you take a step back and critically evaluate yourself, your region, your division, and/or your team, are you living up to the original commitments made to prospects, now clients?

14 Essential Wholesaling Skills Your Manager Wants You to Have

Ten years ago, I asked an outside vendor to help me and my team put together an assessment that we might be able to use to pre-screen wholesalers at the point of the interview. What I wanted was something that was custom designed.

While DISC and Myers Briggs are instructive, they are not specific to the craft of wholesaling.

The vendor undertook interviews with successful existing wholesalers we employed as well as national sales managers and divisional sales managers within our firm.

The findings were distilled down into two distinct categories. Those skills we deemed to be most critical indicators of success and secondary (though not less important) skills.

The first seven are the critical skills sales managers want wholesalers to have.

1. **Work ethic:** There's a lot I can train someone to be. But I can't train someone not to be lazy.

   No, not the couch potato, "Honey get me another beer" lazy that you might be thinking of.

   Work ethic means you wake up most days ready to kill it.

You want to see six appointments in the day and you only have five booked. Between appointments you are on the phone with reps.

You feel guilty for taking a vacation (Disclaimer: I am not advocating not taking time off but a little guilt never hurt) and work harder when you get back.

You complete assigned tasks before they are due. You … you get the picture, right?

2. **Self-starter:** A kissing cousin of work ethic, this means that you don't wait for answers, processes, or solutions to come to you. Rather, you figure them out.

   Frequently this manifests itself when, as an example, you think about a piece of technology or a piece of literature that you do not have and the competition does.

   The self-starter figures out how to create a work-around, or alternate solution. The rest of the folks complain and whine that they don't have what they need to succeed.

3. **Time management:** If you have a copy of the "15 Sales Rules to Live (and Die) By" (see later in this section), then you know that the number one rule is be on time, every time.

   And time management is even more vital.

   Your administrative reports are completed when (before?) they are due.

   You know how to schedule your travel effectively within your loops.

You make the time to clearly document your meetings in the CRM system.

Your office days are not reduced to a gigantic time suck.

4. **Communication skills:** Great wholesalers understand the art of 360-degree communication.

   This means they know how to effectively communicate with their boss, their peers, and internal partners who do not have the same position (or title, or seniority) in the firm.

   Have you experienced the guy/gal who is a sugar-coated suck-up when they speak to the boss and a raving bitch when they speak to a customer service rep?

   Don't be that person!

   This also means you are adept at the written word as well as the spoken word.

   Think internal emails are a place to skip spell check, write in all lower case, use shorthand [CUL8R]? You're wrong.

   Lastly, check your ability to articulate, enunciate, use pace, silence, volume, and vocabulary to enhance your ability to communicate verbally.

5. **Public speaking:** Yes, I know you think you are a great speaker. Most wholesalers do.

   Some are right. Others, how do I put this delicately, *suck*!

Do yourself a favor and get a critical, non-biased eye on your presentations.

This means what your husband/wife or mom thinks does not count.

6. **Self-discipline:** How many jobs in America give you almost complete autonomy, with company benefits, and allow you to earn north of $250k — at the age of 31?

Well in exchange for that I expect wholesalers to know how to carry themselves.

Who can handle their alcohol.

Who know how to respond to the CEO of a broker/dealer when they meet them.

Who know the rep top producer trip to Kona is not designed as their private, expense-paid getaway.

Who always see and respect the line between client and friend.

7. **Resilience/Tenacity:** This is one of the hardest jobs there is.

Wholesalers frequently get the short-end of the rep stick.

Performance sucks? Blame the wholesaler.

Bad seminar turnout? Blame the wholesaler.

Fight with your wife? Blame the wholesaler.

And through it all great wholesalers just keep showing up, providing great ideas, building consultative relationships, demonstrating every day why that rep/broker/agent/IMO can't afford to do business without them.

Here's my personal guarantee: you perfect these seven, and all of their permutations, and you will never be without a wholesaling gig again.

While the following skills were rated as less critical on a scale of 1-10 than the attributes in the first seven, it should be noted that these all came in very closely behind and are really no less important to the success of the great wholesaler.

8. **Self-confidence:** There is a fine line between self-confident and cocky. Think of it this way: cocky is self-confidence gone bad.

    Yet, underneath all the brash and brazen behavior of the cocky wholesaler there is some form of self-confidence. It's just being masked by this annoying facade of arrogance.

    Conversely the self-confident wholesaler has an assurance about him that is almost palpable. Kind of like, dare I say, Tiger Woods — before the ten alleged mistresses?

9. **Friendliness:** Maybe this should be called "likeability," or are they the same? Folks that have the ability to connect with others quickly, to find points of connection that lead to an immediate dialog, or start to gain trust right out of the gate make for great wholesalers (see "10 Ways Wholesalers Can Increase Their Likeability" in Part One).

10. **Organization:** When I managed wholesalers I had no tolerance for late sales reports, expense reports, etc. My thought was, and is, if I am paying you in excess of $250k per year you can figure out how to get your administrative house in order.

   Attention wholesalers: Want to gain favor with your manager? Do your administrative work on time so he/she doesn't have to nag you like an adolescent child.

11. **Stress tolerance/Deals with change:** This assessment of preferred wholesaler skills was done a number of years ago and I imagine that this attribute would have been on the essentials list if managers were polled today.

   That's because wholesalers today are tested in ways that simply were unthinkable three years ago. Hostile advisors, dissatisfied shareholders/policy owners, and skeptical prospects all make for additional clicks of the stress meter to the right. Add in the rigors of travel, activity tracking, CRM requirements, the number of folks in line to take your job, downsizing, right-sizing, product changes, new marketing campaigns, a new CEO, a new sales manager, higher sales goals, less expense money, and the stress-o-meter has passed maxed out. It's at 11!

   Managers need wholesalers who work well under stress and can deal with change — and a ton of it.

12. **Motivation to change:** Do you take feedback well? What do you do with it? Great wholesalers are introspective and are looking for ways to up their game. They seek out feedback and they act on it.

13. **Socially adept:** Just because you are a market (or marketing) genius does not mean you have the social skills to make it as a great wholesaler.

    Did you hear the one about the wholesaler that popped Xanax before large events just to get through the whole event?

    I knew this wholesaler.

    Not socially adept.

    No longer in the business.

14. **Emotional maturity:** This list isn't just about wholesalers or employees; it's about how we all interact in the world. Not to get too zen (but I am from California …), the partial list of attributes of emotional maturity are:

    - Listening to others without passing judgment
    - Knowing how to fight fair, to argue without making it personal
    - Mastering the art of compromise
    - Seeing, and considering, another person's perspective
    - Expressing your feelings appropriately
    - Taking responsibility for your actions and behaviors

- Maintaining perspective under trying circumstances
- Keeping your word and being dependable
- Having a sense of humor, including self-deprecating humor

So how do you self-assess your skills on these 14 attributes? Where do you have room to grow or improve?

15 Sales Rules to Live (and Die) By

More than 10 years ago, in January 1999, I wrote a memo to a new wholesaling organization that I was starting.

It was designed to set the baseline for how we would carry ourselves and face off against customers.

These rules became the foundation for developing the team's MQ — Memorability Quotient®.

Years later they are all still as relevant as the day I wrote them.

- Don't just be on time, be early.
- Trite but true: Under promise and over deliver … every time.
- If they ask for one of something, send them two.
- If they want it in two days send it in one.
- No sale will ever compromise your integrity.
- No salesperson needs to work with abusive (verbal or otherwise) reps. Take 'em off your list.
- Remove "no," "can't," "won't," etc. from your vocabulary.
- Be the best dressed/most immaculately groomed person at every client meeting. They *will* notice.
- Be a student of the market/business. If you don't subscribe to and read *The Wall Street Journal*,

Forbes, Fortune, Money, Smart Money, Kiplingers, The NY Times, etc., start today.

- Always look for the lighter/brighter side. If you're not having fun and laughing along the way, we need to talk.

- Have you hugged your internal sales partner/admin today, telephonically speaking of course?

- Expand your vocabulary and the clarity of your voice. I may not be the smartest guy around, but I might sound like it!

- Simple math: Salesperson Listen to Talk Ratio = 2:1.

- Creativity sells. If you're feeling brain dead, let's brain storm.

- Be the best prepared salesperson in your territory. If you're winging it you better be real good … or lucky!

 ## Stiletto Heels and Power Washers

We all have our "thing."

One is my frustration dealing with Minimum Required People (MRP).

Another is my disdain for having my car serviced.

I guess it's the fact that I have no idea what's really wrong with the car and all the control is in the hands of the servicer.

That, and it's usually a horrible customer service experience.

Recently, I went to the dealer to have my 2006 Honda Ridgeline pickup (don't judge) serviced.

The Service Writer, a petite young woman (who was fashionably dressed and in stiletto heels) wrote me up and said the car would be ready at 8:30 AM.

As the only thing it required was an oil change, and one of their handy 362-Point Inspections, I decided to wait for the car to be done.

At 8:29 I looked over at the car wash bay — as that's the final step before giving me my car back — and noticed that, since all the other workers were busy, she was washing my truck.

With a power washer.

In her stiletto heels.

My car was handed back to me at 8:30 AM as promised.

Clearly she's not an MRP.

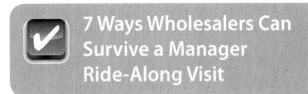

7 Ways Wholesalers Can Survive a Manager Ride-Along Visit

You get the call that your manager is coming to town and expects to ride shotgun with you for three days.

Most wholesalers have a mixture of emotions.

Dread: No one likes to have their performance evaluated in the act of performing. This is especially true if your sales numbers have not been up to snuff.

Anxiety: Will you make the right impression? Will all of your planned activities actually happen and not get canceled? Will you get lost on the way to a rep's office?

Relief: You've been waiting for the boss to arrive and look forward to their coaching.

Excitement: There are COIs (Centers of Influence) that the boss should meet and will help position you in a still better light with them.

Whatever your feelings about this impending visit, here are some points to not overlook.

1. **Run the boss into the ground:** You heard it right. This is not the three appointments a day and a round of golf on Friday summer schedule. If the boss is coming they expect to see you at your best — and that

includes a full calendar. Shoot for five appointments per day.

2. **Vary the kind of appointments:** Show the boss that you are great in all settings. Schedule appointments that are lunch meetings, branch training sessions, group presentations, one on ones, etc.

3. **Introduce them to COIs:** Use the boss's visit to get in front of the COIs that have been resistant to see you. Tell the COI that your boss comes bearing information about the relationship with his firm from a more holistic vantage point and that the COI would benefit from the discussion.

4. **Get the boss in front of your best clients:** Top producers always want to feel loved. One great way to say "you're damn important" is to make sure that when a big-wig comes to town they are able to kiss the top producer's ring.

5. **Make sure there is scheduled one-on-one time:** If your boss doesn't suggest it, you should. Make sure there is time for you to get feedback about your performance and where the opportunities for improvement could be. No one is above feedback (see "How Valuable Is Candid Feedback?" in Part Three).

6. **Ask them to present at a group meeting:** Not to do your job for you but to learn from them. Assuming their skill level exceeds yours, why not put them into action.

7. **Remember the small stuff:** No, you are not a suck-up. Yes, you are a great host. Pick them up at the airport. Drop them at the hotel. Have meals pre-arranged/reservations made. Clean your car (including your trunk!). Fill your tank with gas. Shine your shoes.

True story: Some years ago, I was riding with a brand new wholesaler I hired, and we were approaching a busy toll booth on the I-294.

He pulls up to the exact change coin bin and frantically searches for *any* money. Then he looks at me with sheer terror in his eyes as the docile citizens of Chicago, stacking up behind us, began to lose their patience.

Panicked, he literally was frozen in place at the toll plaza.

I get out and beg the car behind us to take $1 in return for two quarters.

Lesson Learned: Be ready for everything and overlook nothing when your manager is coming for a ride-a-along.

So many of my coaching clients lament the fact that the boss never shows up and, if they do, that the visit was unproductive.

***Are you ready to take matters into your
own hands when your boss visits?***

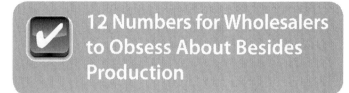

12 Numbers for Wholesalers to Obsess About Besides Production

Are wholesalers focused on the wrong numbers?

No, I have not lost my mind.

Yes, dollars in the door — gross tonnage — is still the measurement of success for virtually most wholesalers.

But what if production is the wrong number to focus on every single day?

Unlike sales professions where we control the end buyer, we only get to attempt to influence the intermediary.

That means we can't walk away from a day's work knowing that we sold a car, a container, or a house.

So, instead of obsessing about how much business we need to do daily to meet our monthly goal and our annual goal, what about eating the elephant (your goal) in more bite-sized pieces?

You eat the elephant instead of the elephant eating you.

Try setting goals for:

1. Number of appointments daily
2. Number of appointments weekly
3. Number of new prospects seen weekly

4. Number of hypos or illustrations run weekly

5. Number of drop-ins attempted weekly

6. Number of branch meetings weekly

7. Number of social events weekly

8. Number of referrals requested weekly

9. Number of successful forward schedules (see "Advanced Wholesaler Technique: The Benefits of Forward Scheduling" in Part Three) completed weekly

10. Number of thank you calls completed weekly

11. Number of thank you notes (email or snail-mail) completed weekly

12. Number of client events scheduled (see "23 Client Event Ideas for Wholesalers to Use with Advisors" in Part Two) monthly

This much is true: if you take care of the numbers, then the numbers will take care of you.

So, if you diligently and thoughtfully goal set around these numbers — and hit these goals with regularity — the production will follow.

I never have seen it not.

Until the time when the production numbers fall in line, you get to celebrate success each and every time you meet or exceed these goals.

And celebrating success feels good.

And when you feel good, you do good.

Mojo anyone?

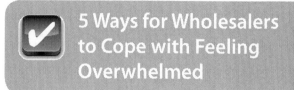
Wholesalers are *busy* folks.

Scheduling your appointments.

Making travel plans.

Ordering the necessary literature.

Preparing winning presentations.

Traveling to appointments.

Meeting with advisors.

Taking/making endless phone calls.

Reading/responding to floods of emails.

CRM data entry of your appointments.

Sending follow-up correspondence.

Responding to home office/manager special requests.

And the other countless business tasks (not to mention the stuff going on in your personal life) that cause even the greatest wholesalers to feel, at times, completely overwhelmed.

So what's a wholesaler to do?

What allows you to mitigate the noise and decompress from the insanity?

1. **Invest in admin assistance.**

   Have you ever calculated your hourly wage?

   At $250k per year (depending on the number of hours a week you work) it's north of $100 per hour.

   That's a lot of money for administrative work.

   Check out sites like HireMyMom or elance, and you'll be amazed at the quality of help you can find at prices that will surprise you.

   In fact, that's how I found my assistant Wendy — and she's awesome.

   If you had to spend an extra $500 per month to make an extra $50,000 a year, isn't that money well spent?

   Not ready for that leap?

   Then use technology more effectively.

   Explore Dragon Dictation to dictate call notes for cut/paste into CRM.

   Both CamCard and CardMunch (a LinkedIn product) allow for effective tracking and handling of business cards collected at conferences and larger rep events.

2. **Make a list.**

   Sure it sounds basic — and it works.

   Just the fact that you can get all the thoughts that are swirling in your brain out onto a real or virtual piece of paper helps relieve the overwhelmed feeling.

I use both a simple spiral-bound loose-leaf notebook (which, once filled, is always saved and filed by date) for bigger projects and online note services/to dos for daily/weekly task reminders.

Apps/sites like Evernote, Fetchnotes, Toodledo are all used by wholesalers to effectively get a handle on the endless stream of things to be done.

3. **Me (you) time.**

   Your clients, prospects, internals, boss, spouse, kids, friends, acquaintances, social networking pals, etc., all require bits and pieces of your precious time.

   So, where is your "you" time?

   Make a commitment to yourself to:

   - Go get a massage
   - Take a long solo bike ride
   - Go for a run
   - Sit on a bench
   - Walk around a city and take photos (one of my favorites that I've recently started to chronicle on Pinterest)
   - Read a non-business book
   - Stare at a wall

   It doesn't matter what the what is — it matters that you take time for you.

4. **Remove tolerations from your life.**

   In the Fall 2011 edition of *I Carry The Bag*, life coach Mary Allen talked about the importance of removing tolerations from your list of life's daily to dos.

   What are tolerations?

   They're the little items that pile up in our lives and take up space in our thoughts — space that can be freed up for more impactful/important items.

   It's everything from that errand you keep meaning to run to the household item you keep meaning to get repaired.

5. **Get more comfortable with the word "no."**

   We are wired to say "yes" as much as possible because as sales professionals we feel we might miss something if we say no.

   And the truth is you have to say no from time to time … even though it may never feel good to say it.

   However, your ability to say no, to find alternative solutions and navigate creative outcomes will most certainly lessen the weight of feeling overwhelmed.

   ***What do you do to get past the feeling
   of being overwhelmed?***

6 Ways Wholesalers Become Franchise Players

The days of the lone wolf wholesaler are dead.

That's right, the wholesalers that profess the credo of "I just want to be left alone to do my job" have become extinct as quickly as the Antillean Giant Rice Rat.

Welcome to the age of the franchise player.

Franchise players (FPs) are wholesalers who:

1. Understand the greater objectives and goals of the firm. This means that during the next meeting where your boss (or higher) is outlining the strategy for the next year and the tactics that will get your firm there, FPs are actually paying attention and absorbing the message.

2. Look upon partner departments (marketing, sales support, service and, yes, legal/compliance) as colleagues and not forces of evil. In fact, real FPs are the wholesalers who volunteer to have representatives of these partner departments ride with them so that they might learn the real challenges of wholesaling from the best place possible — your passenger seat.

3. Welcome the reciprocal nature of others seeking to gain entry to your contacts. In firms that have wholesaler segments such as retirement plans, variable

account, ETF, defined benefit, A&H, etc., FPs see the "big round world" benefit of cross-pollinating.

4. Take time to mentor newer members of the whole-saling team who will benefit from their sage advice.

5. Place high regard on the training and development of internal (and hybrid) partners. FPs relish the chance to positively influence the next wave of great wholesalers.

6. Have influential relationships with their boss. FPs are valuable contributors to the future direction of the sales team because they have the ability to offer both candid and constructive feedback to their boss.

Nobody expects the sheer number of wholesaling professionals to return to the pre-2008 days.

And, it's a certainty that our profession will be tested again by the next flash crash, terrorist attack, economic downturn, or political malaise.

It's also a certainty that Franchise Players generally don't get cut or traded.

Are you a franchise player or ready to be put on waivers?

8 Ways Great Wholesalers Prepare for Vacation

Beaches.

Sightseeing.

Adult beverages at breakfast.

That's right — it's time for my annual week off.

Yet in order to make sure that I was actually able to decompress a little, I needed to prepare for vacation — and not just the airfare, hotel, and rental car reservations.

Here are the eight ways that you should prepare too.

1. Call all of your top producers in advance of your trip to let them know you'll be gone.
2. Have a backup in place (another external wholesaler or your boss).
3. Make sure your out-of-office email and voice mail is properly in place.
4. Cover your bases with the home office folks who need to know.
5. Notify your best/highest profile prospects.
6. Tee up an email to be sent while you are away.
7. Send a snail-mail campaign while you are gone.
8. Make sure your internal has explicit instructions about what's to be done while you are gone.

Who ever said taking time off was easy?

Necessary, yes.

Easy, no.

Do you properly prepare your practice for vacations?

 Confessions of a Hotel Snob

Back in the early 2000s I was down in Macon, GA, riding with a wholesaler.

We put in a full day of five solid appointments, then a dinner, and it was time to find the hotel for the night.

And that's where it got ugly.

My experience via these six signs confirmed, yet again, that I am a bona fide hotel snob.

1. The registration *window* was just off of the parking lot.
2. The doors to the rooms all faced outward, toward the same parking lot.
3. The front desk clerk had an economy of teeth.
4. The room was prepaid before the key was released to the guest.

5. The pillows on the bed were more roundish —
   and made of foam.

6. The bed squeaked at the slightest move.

Safe travels!

11 Reasons Great Wholesalers Leap Out of Bed in the Morning

You and I both know that wholesaling is one of the best gigs ever created.

But I'll bet some mornings it just doesn't seem like it.

Some mornings you wake up and simply aren't looking forward to another trip to the airport, more traffic, another advisor who is barely listening, or another branch training session.

I've been asking some of my coaching clients what makes them leap out of bed and the partial list looks like this.

1. **Money:** If this isn't on your list please tell me what is. 100% of wholesalers that I have spoken to over the last 25 years have money and recognition ranked in their top three reasons for living this life called wholesaler.

2. **Recognition:** Where were you on the Leader Board today? How did your sales rank in the division last month? Have you received an attaboy from your boss, a colleague, or a client recently? Some of my clients place recognition ahead of money when it comes to the things that get them charged up and keep them running.

3. **Competition:** Great wholesalers simply get a thrill out of squashing their competition. Yes, they always handle product comparisons with class and never throw stones at their fellow wholesaler. They do, however, thrive on taking market share away from anyone who dares challenge their position with a single advisor, in a branch/office, or at a firm.

4. **Family:** Arguably this is the strongest motivator for wholesalers with a significant other, and especially with children. We have assumed an amazing amount of responsibility for the care and feeding of those who count on us to provide. For some it is all the reason they need to leap out of bed and light it up — every day.

5. **The game:** This was how one client depicted the advisor/wholesaler relationship. He said that it was analogous to chess — making sure that your wholesaler "moves" were properly planned and executed so as to maximize both the relationship with the advisor and the amount of business you are able to earn.

6. **Creativity:** Yes, we work in a highly regulated world. But that doesn't mean that creativity needs to go out the window. Great wholesalers stay engaged by always modifying, even if subtly, their product pitch, platform skills, sales ideas, etc.

7. **Curiosity:** Who's the new manager at the branch in Midtown? Why was the recent product change priced that way? As I analyze my business, why are so many clients married and over 50? An innate need to ask

questions is a hallmark of wholesalers that stay engaged.

8. **Thrill of the hunt:** Who doesn't get a buzz from closing the deal? You learn of a new rep in your region, schedule an appointment to go see them, hit it off, provide great information, add much more than product to the relationship, close for the business and are rewarded with a million-dollar producer. Thrilling indeed!

9. **Fear:** We all know that the greatest motivators are fear and greed. To debate which is more powerful is fruitless. To know that there is nothing wrong with healthy doses of fear (versus paranoia) to propel your engagement is to be honest with yourself. After all, we are all afraid of something.

10. **Ego:** While a blend of some of the other drivers mentioned, it still deserves a mention of its own. Many years ago, I was given a button that read "Where Ego, I Go Too." True.

11. **Helping:** The simple and unadulterated great feeling that comes from knowing that you, your product, and your firm make a difference to the advisor and their end client.

So, what keeps you engaged?
Why get up and fight the next battle?

CONCLUSION

 Your Picture of Success

What does success look like to you?

Is it measured in dollars and cents?

Or is it defined by examining the leader board at your firm?

What goals stand before you in the next 365 days?

How will you insure that the year ahead will be your year?

The one in which you break through.

The one in which you conquer.

The one in which your picture of success is in clear, full, bright, living color.

The good news: the wholesaling clock can start anew starting today.

The bad news: only a small percentage of folks will edit their picture, even after reading this far.

The canvas is blank.

Go make the rest of your career a beautiful picture of success.

After 200+ posts at WholesalerMasterminds.com, more than 50 Wholesaler Masterminds Radio shows, 3 years of publishing *I Carry The Bag*, and working with thousands of wholesalers, there is one thing of which I am certain.

We've only scratched the surface of the required knowledge, skills, and subtle nuances required for you to have a wholesaling career that provides you and your family with all of the rewards that you seek.

Let me know how I can assist you in creating your picture of success.

For the latest articles, podcasts,
and videos be sure to visit

Wholesaler Masterminds®
WHERE GOOD WHOLESALERS BECOME GREAT WHOLESALERS

at

www.wholesalermasterminds.com

ABOUT THE AUTHOR

Rob Shore has over 30 years' experience in Financial Services, with 25 of those years spent in Distribution. His proven background in corporate America has provided him with a reputation as a leader who has been recognized for innovation, results, creativity, and, most importantly, extraordinary sales success.

Rob was part of the "new wave" of brokers in banks circa 1987 and he cut his wholesaling teeth at Oppenheimer-Funds where he helped build Oppenheimer's early entry into bank distribution and as one of the channel's founding wholesalers — and where he maintained the #1 wholesaling rank for four consecutive years.

Later, as President of Allstate Distributors, L.L.C., he led the activities of cross-channel product distribution and marketing that produced over $30 billion in top line sales and achieved 30% annual compounded sales growth.

Today he is the CEO of shorespeak, L.L.C., which publishes WholesalerMasterminds.com, the defacto online destination for financial services wholesaling professionals, and *I Carry The Bag* magazine, the official magazine of wholesaling.

He is a frequent speaker at national sales conferences and divisional meetings and spends most days coaching his private and group wholesaling and leadership coaching clients.

He lives with his wife, and a gaggle of small domestic animals, in the California wine country.

ABOUT THE COVER

When it was purchase back in the early 1990s, this Tumi brief-case was about the most expensive item in my professional arsenal. Throughout the years it has seen almost 2 million air miles, over 250,000 road miles, and countless advisor appointments.

The original bag that I carried is pictured on the cover of this book.

Oh, if briefcases could talk …

Made in the USA
Middletown, DE
01 March 2016